Eyewitness
PLANT

Blackberries

Red ginseng root

Gerbera flower

Moss on decaying wood

Radish

Peppers

Ornamental dried corn

Ribwort plantain seed heads

Opium poppy seed heads

Redshank flowers

Delphinium
flowers

Eyewitness
PLANT

pansy
p...

Written by
DAVID BURNIE

Garden yarrow
flower head

Columbine
seed heads

ster

Feverfew
flowers

DK

DK Publishing, Inc.

Ripe fig cut
in half

Poppy
seed
head

Eucalyptus
leaves

Fi
scabi

...on sorrel

Creeping
crowfoot

DK

LONDON, NEW YORK, MELBOURNE,
MUNICH, and DELHI

Project editor Helen Parker
Senior editor Sophie Mitchell
Senior art editor Julia Harris
Managing editor Sue Unstead
Managing art editor Roger Priddy
Special photography
Andrew McRobb of the Royal Botanic Gardens, Kew
Karl Shone, Kim Taylor, and Jane Burton
Editorial consultants
The staff of the Natural History Museum, London
and the Royal Botanic Gardens, Kew

Yarrow
leaf

Cow
vetch

PAPERBACK EDITION
Managing editor Andrew Macintyre
Managing art editor Jane Thomas
Editor Karen O'Brien
Art editor Ann Cannings
Production Jenny Jacoby
Picture research Lorna Ainger
DTP designer Siu Yin Ho

U.S. editor Elizabeth Hester
Senior editor Beth Sutinis
Art director Dirk Kaufman
U.S. production Chris Avgherinos
U.S. DTP designer Milos Orlovic

This Eyewitness ® Guide has been conceived by
Dorling Kindersley Limited and Editions Gallimard

This edition published in the United States in 2004
by DK Publishing, Inc., 375 Hudson Street, New York, NY 10014

07 08 10 9 8 7 6 5 4

Copyright © 1989, © 2004 Dorling Kindersley Limited.

A catalog record for this book is available from the Library of Congress.
ISBN-13: 978-0-7566-0715-9 (PLC)
ISBN-13: 978-0-7566-0714-2 (ALB)

Color reproduction by Colourscan, Singapore
Printed in China by Toppan Printing Co. (Shenzhen), Ltd.

Common
toadflax

Oxeye
daisy

Discover more at
www.dk.com

Cuckoo-
pint

Flower
of blue
echeveria

Bull
thistle

Contents

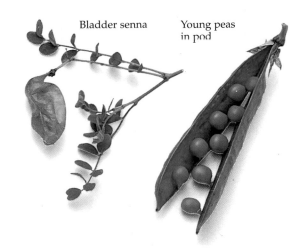

Bladder senna   Young peas in pod

What is a plant?

Plants are the key to life on Earth. Without them many other living organisms would soon disappear. This is because higher life forms depend on plants, either directly or indirectly, for their food. Most plants, however, are able to make their own food using sunlight. All plants fall into two basic categories. Flowering plants, which this book looks at in some detail, produce true flowers. The nonflowering plants include "primitive" plants, such as mosses, ferns, horsetails, and liverworts, and the gymnosperms, a group of plants which includes the conifers, like the giant sequoias, shown opposite. There are about a quarter of a million species of flowering plants in the world today, and they grow almost everywhere from snowy mountain slopes to arid deserts. This book tells their story.

Lichen

THIS IS NOT A PLANT
It is often difficult to tell simple plants and animals apart. This plantlike organism is a hydrozoan and lives in the sea. Its "branches" are formed by tiny animals called polyps, which have tentacles to trap particles of food.

THIS IS A PLANT
A lichen is made up of two different organisms: a tiny nonflowering plant called an alga, and a fungus. The algal cells live among the tiny threads formed by the fungus and supply the fungus with food, which they make using sunlight (pp. 14-15). The fungus cannot make its own food and would die without the alga. Lichens grow very slowly and are extremely long-lived.

Licher
growing c
limestone roc

THIS WAS A PLANT
Forests of horsetails and giant club-mosses, up to 150 ft (45 m) tall, once formed a large part of the Earth's vegetation (right). Over 300 million years, their remains have turned into coal.

Horsetail

MODERN RELATIONS
Ferns and horsetails are primitive plants that do not have flowers but reproduce by spores. Both first appeared nearly 300 million years ago. Although there are still many types of fern, only 30 species of horsetail live on Earth today.

Spores

Hart's-tongue fern

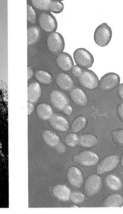

THE BIGGEST AND THE SMALLEST
The world's most massive plants are conifers – the giant sequoias of California, which can reach heights of over 310 ft (95 m). The smallest flowering plant is the rootless duckweed which is 0.01 in (0.3 mm) across.

Ribbon-like "thallus" divides into branches as it grows

Garden pansy

LIVERWORTS
Liverworts are nonflowering plants that live in damp places and reproduce by means of spores.

MOSSES
Mosses do not have flowers. Like liver-worts, they reproduce by means of tiny spores.

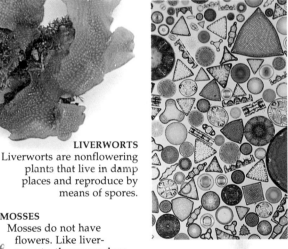

LIVING SCULPTURES
Algae are simple, non-flowering plants. A diatom is a single-celled alga which has a rigid trans-parent case, or frustule, made of silica, a glasslike substance. This microscope photograph shows many species of diatom, each of which has a frustule of a different shape and pattern.

FLOWERING PLANTS
Unlike the other plants on these two pages, these have true flowers. They are also unique in having seeds which develop inside a protective structure called an ovary (p. 17). This later develops into a fruit (pp. 26-27). The garden pansy is a typical flowering plant.

GREEN BLANKETS
Some species of aqua-tic algae form long chains of cells, creating slimy blanket-weed.

Spirogyra blanket-weed

The parts of a plant

FLOWERING PLANTS ARE BUSY throughout the day and nigh
During the hours of daylight, the leaves collect th
sun's energy. The plant then uses this energy t
create food, in the form of sugars (pp. 14-15). Th
second process is carried out in the dark. A
the food is produced, it has to be transporte
away from the leaves to the places where it
needed. At the same time, water and mineral
which the roots have absorbed from the soi
have to be carried in the opposite directio
to the farthest stems and branches. Re:
piration - the way in which the plar
breathes - occurs throughout the 2
hours, just as in animals. As the plar
matures, it embarks on the com
plicated process of growing flower
producing and receiving polle
and eventually scattering seec

Lateral roots

Fine root hairs near the tip of each rootlet absorb water and minerals from the soil

Woody lower stem contai "lignin," which makes it stro

Main root divides to anchor plant in ground

Small shoots th sprout around t base of a larg plant are known adventitious shoo or sucke

Lateral root

Main root

New later ro

Xylem carries water upward

Root growth occurs at the tip of each root

LOOKING THROUG A ROC
In a root, the tub
like cells that condu
water, minerals, •
sugars are grouped
the center. As a ro
grows, other smaller roo
branch off it, helping
absorb water and nutrien
and anchoring the plant
the ground. All roots have
cap of slimy cells at their ti
These cells prevent the roots fro
being worn away as they gro
through the groun

Phloem carries food to growing tip of root

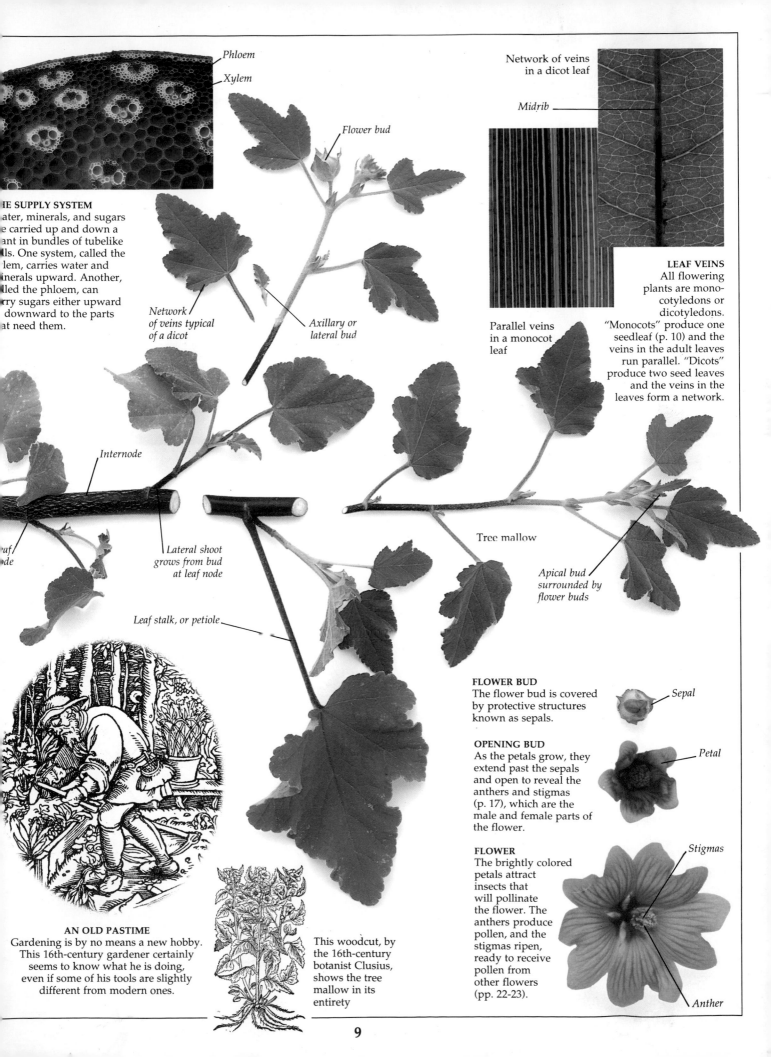

Phloem

Xylem

HE SUPPLY SYSTEM
ater, minerals, and sugars
e carried up and down a
ant in bundles of tubelike
lls. One system, called the
lem, carries water and
inerals upward. Another,
lled the phloem, can
rry sugars either upward
downward to the parts
at need them.

Flower bud

Network of veins typical of a dicot

Axillary or lateral bud

Network of veins in a dicot leaf

Midrib

LEAF VEINS
All flowering
plants are mono-
cotyledons or
dicotyledons.
"Monocots" produce one
seedleaf (p. 10) and the
veins in the adult leaves
run parallel. "Dicots"
produce two seed leaves
and the veins in the
leaves form a network.

Parallel veins
in a monocot
leaf

Internode

Lateral shoot grows from bud at leaf node

Tree mallow

Apical bud surrounded by flower buds

Leaf stalk, or petiole

AN OLD PASTIME
Gardening is by no means a new hobby.
This 16th-century gardener certainly
seems to know what he is doing,
even if some of his tools are slightly
different from modern ones.

This woodcut, by
the 16th-century
botanist Clusius,
shows the tree
mallow in its
entirety

FLOWER BUD
The flower bud is covered
by protective structures
known as sepals.

Sepal

OPENING BUD
As the petals grow, they
extend past the sepals
and open to reveal the
anthers and stigmas
(p. 17), which are the
male and female parts of
the flower.

Petal

FLOWER
The brightly colored
petals attract
insects that
will pollinate
the flower. The
anthers produce
pollen, and the
stigmas ripen,
ready to receive
pollen from
other flowers
(pp. 22-23).

Stigmas

Anther

A plant is born

A SEED IS A TINY LIFE-SUPPORT PACKAGE. Inside it is an embryo, which consists of the basic parts from which the seedling will develop, together with a supply of food. The food is needed to keep the embryo alive and fuel the process of germination (growth). It is either packed around the embryo, in an endosperm, or stored in special seed leaves, known as cotyledons. For weeks, months, or even years, the seed may remain inactive. But then, when the conditions are right, it suddenly comes alive and begins to grow. During germination the seed absorbs water, the cells of the embryo start to divide, and eventually the seed case, or testa, breaks open. First, the beginning of the root system, or radicle, sprouts and grows downward, followed rapidly by the shoot, or plumule, which will produce the stem and leaves.

First true leaves open out

Terminal bud surrounded by next pair of leaves

TINY BUT STRONG
When plants grow, they can exert great pressure. Some seedlings can easily push through the tar on the surface of a new road.

First true leaves

Bent plumule

Seed coat, or testa, containing seed leaves

Plumule straightens toward light

First roots grow downward

3 HARNESSING THE SUN
With the opening of the first true leaves, the seedling starts to produce its own food by photosynthesis (pp. 14-15). Until this time, its growth is fueled entirely by the food reserves stored in the seed leaves.

1 GETTING GOING
The seed of a scarlet runner will germinate only if it is dark and damp. First the skin of the seed splits. The beginning of the root system, the radicle, appears and grows downward. Shortly after this, a shoot appears, initially bent double with its tip buried in the seed leaves. This shoot, or plumule, will produce the stem and leaves.

2 REACHING FOR THE LIGHT
As the plumule grows longer, it breaks above ground. Once it is above the soil, it straightens up toward the light, and the first true leaves appear. In the scarlet runner, the seed leaves stay buried. This is known as "hypogeal" germination. In plants that have "epigeal" germination, such as the sunflower, the seed leaves are lifted above ground, where they turn green and start to produce food for the seedling.

Main root grows deeper

Root hairs absorb water and salts from the soil

First pair of leaves, now fully grown

Leaf stalk

heat is a monocot (p. 9)
cause it has just one seed
f. The young shoot
ows upward through the
l, protected by a tube
led a coleoptile. As with
grasses, the growing point,
apical meristem, of the
ves of the wheat plant is
ground level and can
ntinue to produce new
oots at the base of the
nt even if the leaves are
moved. This is why pasture
n survive being nibbled by
ws, and why lawns thrive
being mown. Other plants,
ch as the bean, have their
owing region, or meristem,
ar the tip. If they are
own or nibbled, they
ust grow out from side
ds instead.

Radicle

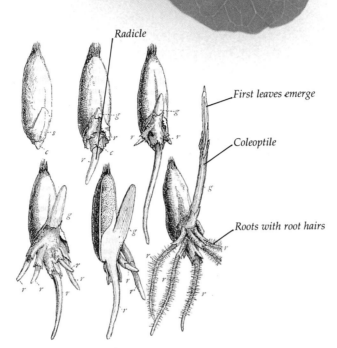

First leaves emerge

Coleoptile

Roots with root hairs

Fully upright stem

Seed case is now not needed and starts to shrivel

4 THE RACE TO REPRODUCE
Once germination is complete, the scarlet runner
grows quickly. Because it is a climbing plant, it does not
need to develop thick stems. Instead, it uses other plants
for support (p. 38). Given the right conditions, the plant
will produce its first flowers in about six weeks.
After pollination (pp. 22-23) and fertilization,
these will develop into long pods full of seeds.
By the time the seeds have dried out, the life
cycle of the scarlet runner has turned full circle.

Thick mass of roots absorbs
water and nutrients from soil

Leaves develop from
underground tuber

A YEARLY CYCLE
Some plants produce
underground storage
organs, such as bulbs,
tubers, and corms
(pp. 32-33). Every
autumn the leaves
of the cuckoopint
die, but the
following spring
new leaves de-
velop from buds
on the tuber.
Although this
process may
look like ger-
mination, it is
very different.

Bursting into bloom

PLANT LOVERS ARE OFTEN PUZZLED as to why, try as they might, they cannot get their houseplants to flower. A plant may be covered in blooms when it is bought, but the following year it will often produce nothing but a mass of green leaves. The reason is that nursery owners treat plants in a particular way to make them flower. All plants have a special control mechanism that makes sure their flowers develop and open at exactly the right time of year. The main factor in bringing a plant to bloom is the length of the night. Some plants will flower only when the nights are long and the days are short (short-day plants). The chrysanthemum, for example, will not flower at all if it is grown indoors in a position where it gets natural light by day and artificial light at night. Other plants, especially those that live far from the equator, flower only at the height of summer, when the days are long. Some flower in any day-length. Once a flower has opened, other mechanisms come into play. Many flowers turn so that they are always facing the sun; others close up every night and reopen in the morning.

Petals folded back

New petals unfolding outward

Petal *Sepal*

THE FLOWER OPENS
The garden nasturtium belongs to a family of plants that comes from South America. When the light conditions are right for the plant, flower buds begin to form. Each flower bud is protected by five sepals. As the bud starts to burst, the sepals open to reveal five bright orange petals which grow outward and fold back. One of the sepals develops a long spur which lies at the back of the flower. This spur produces the nectar that attracts insect pollinators to the flower.

BLOOMING LOVELY
Markings called honey guides show insects the way to the nectar. To reach it, they have to clamber over the anthers (p. 17), which dust them with pollen. As the days pass, the anthers wither and the three stigmas (p. 17) are ready to receive the pollen of other plants. Insects in search of nectar now dust the stigmas with pollen.

The life cycles of plants

Flowering plants have very different life spans, ranging from months to centuries. A common poppy will germinate, flower, scatter seed, and die all within a single year. Plants that live in this way are known as annuals. Other plants, such as the wild carrot (p. 55), take two years to complete the same process. They flower only in their second year - the first is spent growing and building up food reserves, which they store in a thick, fleshy root. These plants are known as biennials. Perennial plants are those that live for a number of years. They include species such as the dandelion (pp. 30-31). Perennial weeds are a particular problem for gardeners because their long life span gives them time to grow very wide-spreading roots.

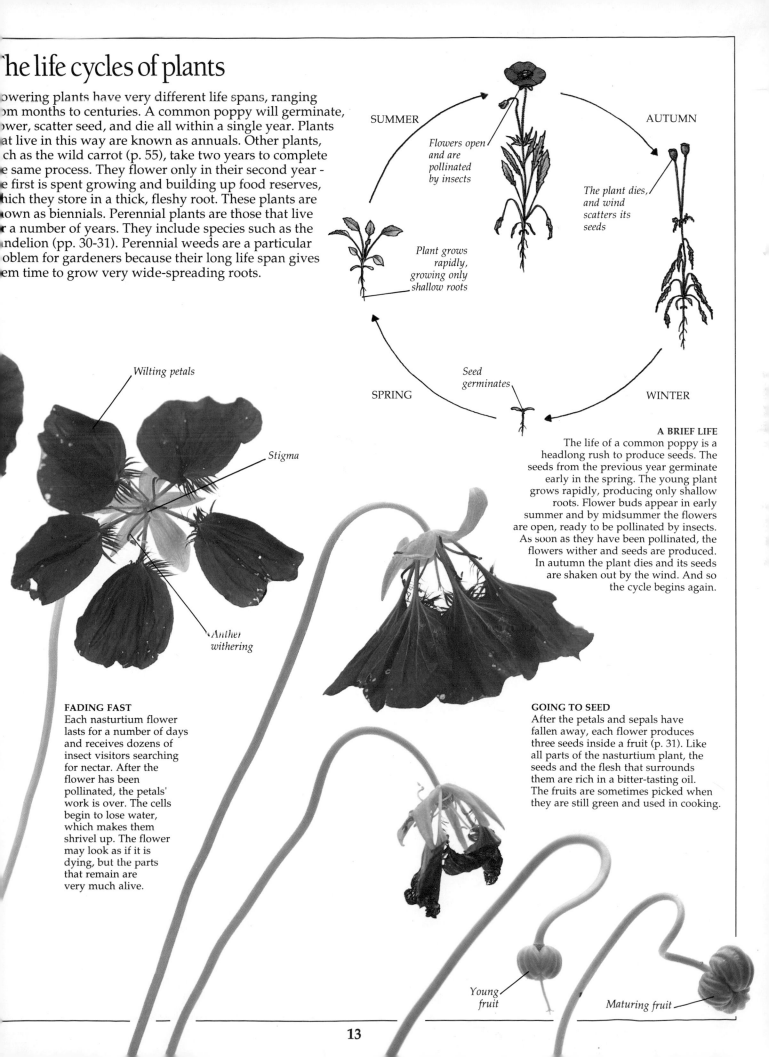

SUMMER

*Flowers open
and are
pollinated
by insects*

AUTUMN

*The plant dies,
and wind
scatters its
seeds*

*Plant grows
rapidly,
growing only
shallow roots*

*Seed
germinates*

SPRING

WINTER

Wilting petals

Stigma

*Anther
withering*

A BRIEF LIFE
The life of a common poppy is a headlong rush to produce seeds. The seeds from the previous year germinate early in the spring. The young plant grows rapidly, producing only shallow roots. Flower buds appear in early summer and by midsummer the flowers are open, ready to be pollinated by insects. As soon as they have been pollinated, the flowers wither and seeds are produced. In autumn the plant dies and its seeds are shaken out by the wind. And so the cycle begins again.

FADING FAST
Each nasturtium flower lasts for a number of days and receives dozens of insect visitors searching for nectar. After the flower has been pollinated, the petals' work is over. The cells begin to lose water, which makes them shrivel up. The flower may look as if it is dying, but the parts that remain are very much alive.

GOING TO SEED
After the petals and sepals have fallen away, each flower produces three seeds inside a fruit (p. 31). Like all parts of the nasturtium plant, the seeds and the flesh that surrounds them are rich in a bitter-tasting oil. The fruits are sometimes picked when they are still green and used in cooking.

*Young
fruit*

Maturing fruit

13

A light diet

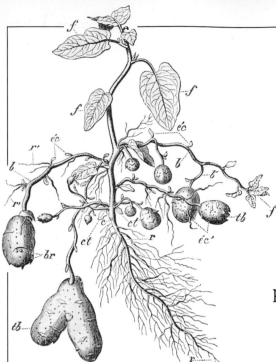

UNLIKE ANIMALS, most plants do not need to find foo because they can make it for themselves. The key to the w they do this lies in a green pigment called chlorophyll, whi gives them their characteristic green color. By means chlorophyll, plants can convert energy from sunlight in chemical energy which can be stored, usually in the form starch, and used to fuel the growth and development of t plant. The light energy is used to convert carbon dioxide a water into an energy-rich food compound called glucose. Th process, known as photosynthesis, works kind of like a bonfi in reverse. If you throw a log onto the fire, the carbon that contained in compounds in the log is reconverted into carb dioxide gas, and the stored energy is released in the form heat and ligh

UNDERGROUND STORAGE

Potatoes are swollen underground stems, known as tubers, which store the food produced by photosynthesis. This food, in the form of starches, provides the young shoots, which develop from buds on the tuber, with enough fuel to enable them to grow quickly. Potatoes also provide an important source of human food and they have been bred to produce bigger tubers.

Leaves produced in the dark have little chlorophyll, leaving them pale, or etiolated

Potato tuber k in dark for mor

Stems grow upward against gravity

A PLANT WITHOUT LIGHT

This potato has spent six months with very little light - a condition that would kill many plants. Because it has been in almost complete darkness, it has not been able to produce any food by photosynthesis. However, it has survived and has even produced some roots and shoots. To do this, the young potato shoots have drawn on the food reserves stored by the parent plant during the previous year's growth. The parent plant used the sun's energy to make food, which it stored in the potato tubers mostly in the form of grains of starch. The young potato plants use the starch to release energy for growth.

Each stem is produced by a small bud, or eye

Adventitious roots

Tuber begins to shrink as food stores are used up

14

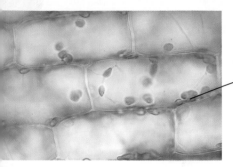

*Chloroplasts
in cells collect
sunlight*

LANT'S SOLAR PANELS

de the cells that make up a plant's leaves
tiny structures called chloroplasts. In a
gle cell, there may be up to a hundred of
m. It is inside the chloroplasts that the
en, light-trapping pigment chlorophyll is
e found. The chloroplasts work like minute
r panels, collecting the sun's energy and
g it to make food.

*Green leaves
rich in
chlorophyll*

STORING SUGAR

Plants store food in various
ways - as starches, sugars,
or oils. In its first year, an
onion plant stores sugars in
the onion bulb, which is
made up of swollen leaf
bases around a short-
ened stem. In the
second year, the sugars
in the onion bulb are
used up as the plant
grows and flowers.
Sugars turn brown, or
caramelize, when
they are heated
strongly, which is
why onions darken
when they are fried.

RAPID REVIVAL

Three weeks after emerging from
the dark, the potato plant is
now growing rapidly, and its
leaves have turned green.
This has happened because
more chlorophyll has been
made in the leaves to harness
the energy of the sunlight
falling on them. The
growing potato
plant is now
able to collect enough
light to build up its own
reserves and it no longer
needs the energy stored in
the old tuber. If the potato
were now planted, the
energy gathered by its
leaves would be stored in
new potato tubers, and the
old tuber would shrivel
and die.

*Stems grow
rapidly upward
and turn toward
the light*

*Thickening
root system
with root
hairs*

A simple flower dissected

The simplest flowers have the parts arranged in a circle, or whorl

FLOWERS HAVE BECOME extraordinarily varied during the cours of evolution. Nature has produced them in a tremendous weal of shapes and colors, and to add to this profusion peop have bred flowers that are even more brilliant or bizar than the ones found in the wild. But behind this bafflir array of shapes and sizes there is a common pattern. Fo seed production, all flowers use the same underlyir structures. The lily flower shown on these two pages quite simple - its parts are all separate, and they ca all be clearly seen. They fall into thre groups. The male parts (the stamen produce the pollen; the fema parts (the carpel) produce th ovules, which will eventual become the seeds. Around bo the male and the female parts a sepals and petals which attract i sects. When, as in this lily flower, th sepals and petals look the same, they are known as perianth segments, or tepals.

Stamen

Stigma

Petal from inner whorl

Sepal from outer whorl

When sepals and petals look the same, they are known as perianth segments, or tepals

Stamens and stigma packed tightly together

Tepals protecting male and female parts of flower

THE LILY FAMILY
The lilies and their relatives make up one of the largest families of flowering plants.

HOW A FLOWER BUD OPE
In the lily's flower bud, the male and female parts are pack tightly together inside the protective casing formed by the sep and petals (tepals). The flower bud opens because certain parts it start to grow more quickly than others. The inside of the base each tepal, for example, grows faster than the outside. This forc the tepal to bend outward at the point where it is connected the flower stalk. At the same time, unequal growth along t edges of each tepal makes the folds in it open o

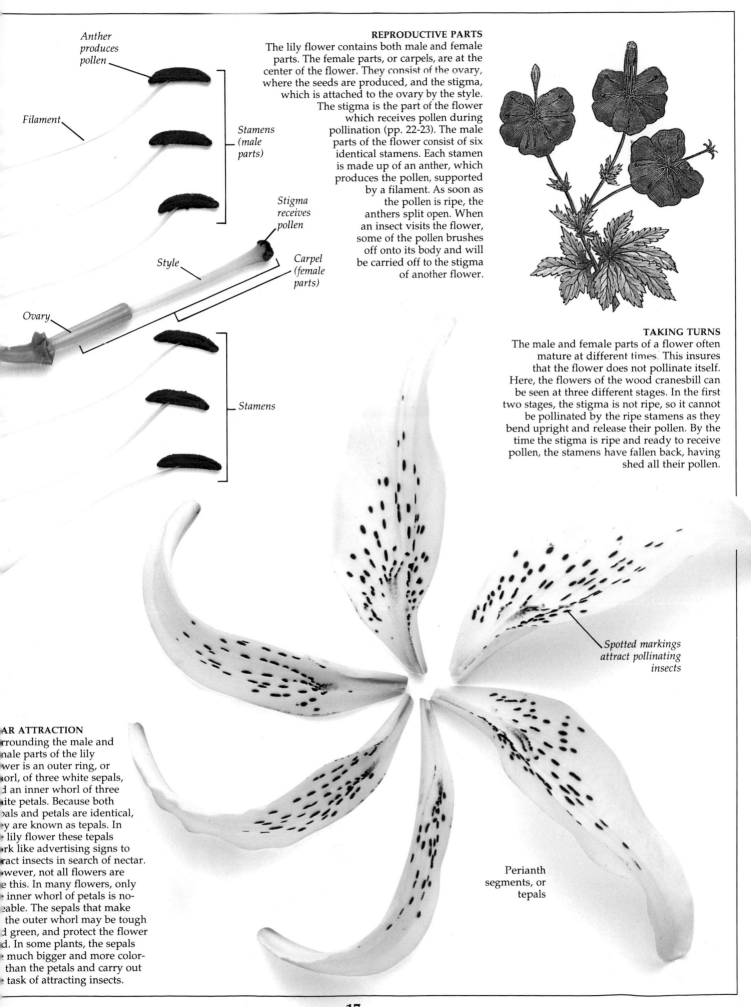

Anther
produces
pollen

Filament

Stamens
(male
parts)

Stigma
receives
pollen

Style

Carpel
(female
parts)

Ovary

Stamens

REPRODUCTIVE PARTS

The lily flower contains both male and female parts. The female parts, or carpels, are at the center of the flower. They consist of the ovary, where the seeds are produced, and the stigma, which is attached to the ovary by the style. The stigma is the part of the flower which receives pollen during pollination (pp. 22-23). The male parts of the flower consist of six identical stamens. Each stamen is made up of an anther, which produces the pollen, supported by a filament. As soon as the pollen is ripe, the anthers split open. When an insect visits the flower, some of the pollen brushes off onto its body and will be carried off to the stigma of another flower.

TAKING TURNS

The male and female parts of a flower often mature at different times. This insures that the flower does not pollinate itself. Here, the flowers of the wood cranesbill can be seen at three different stages. In the first two stages, the stigma is not ripe, so it cannot be pollinated by the ripe stamens as they bend upright and release their pollen. By the time the stigma is ripe and ready to receive pollen, the stamens have fallen back, having shed all their pollen.

Spotted markings
attract pollinating
insects

AR ATTRACTION

rrounding the male and
nale parts of the lily
wer is an outer ring, or
orl, of three white sepals,
d an inner whorl of three
ite petals. Because both
als and petals are identical,
y are known as tepals. In
lily flower these tepals
rk like advertising signs to
ract insects in search of nectar.
wever, not all flowers are
e this. In many flowers, only
inner whorl of petals is no-
able. The sepals that make
the outer whorl may be tough
green, and protect the flower
d. In some plants, the sepals
much bigger and more color-
than the petals and carry out
task of attracting insects.

Perianth
segments, or
tepals

A complex flower

Developing flower bud from the side

Developing nectar spur

THE FLOWERS on these two pages come from the Himalayan balsam. Although they have the same basic parts as the lily flower shown on pages 16-17, evolution has modified them in different ways so that the two flowers look completely different. Compared with the lily flower, the flowers of the balsam are much more complex and specialized. Himalayan balsam flowers are pollinated by long-tongued insects, such as bees, and they are shaped to insure that when the insect approaches and enters the flower, it picks up the grains of pollen from the anthers. Bees are attracted to the flower by sugary nectar which is produced in a spur attached to a pouch at the back of the flower. To reach this nectar, a visiting bee first has to land on a platform made up of petals. It then has to climb right inside the flower and stretch out its long tongue. When the bee is in this position, its back touches the anthers. These give it a dusting of pollen which it then carries to the next flower it visits.

Stigma

Corona threadlike ha

Anther

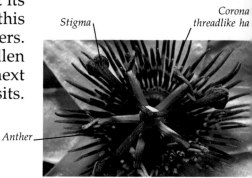

A PAT ON THE BA
Insects visit passionflowers in search of nec produced in the base of the flower. When passionflower opens, the anthers, which lower than the styles (p. 17), dust poll onto the insect's back. A few hours la the styles curve downward so that th are lower than the empty anthers and collect pollen from another insect's ba

Front, or anterior, petal

Flowers develop in clusters and open one at a time

Sepal

Pouch-shaped third sepal

Nectar spur

Two pe joined toget

ATTRACTIVE TO INSECTS
Himalayan balsam flowers each have three sepals and five petals, and are symmetrical (even) insofar as each half is a mirror image of the other. Two of the sepals are small flaps at the base of the flower. They protect the young flower bud. During millions of years of evolution, the third has become much larger and shaped into a pouch. At the end of this pouch lies the narrow spur which produces nectar.

Fully formed flower from the side

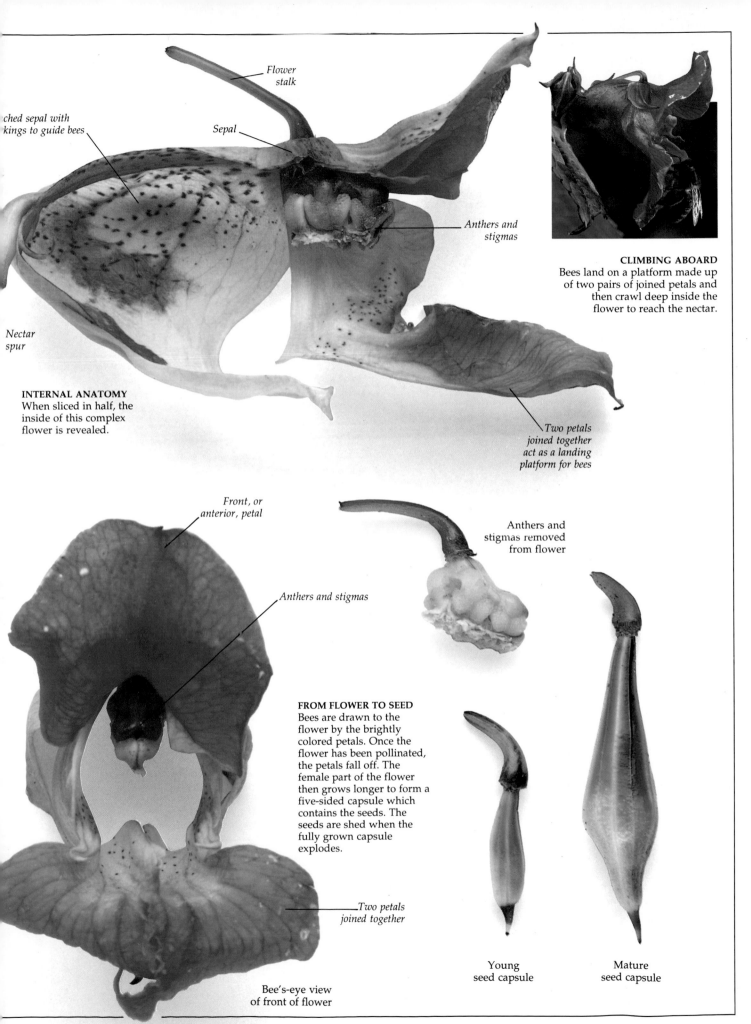

Flower stalk

...ched sepal with ...kings to guide bees

Sepal

Anthers and stigmas

CLIMBING ABOARD
Bees land on a platform made up of two pairs of joined petals and then crawl deep inside the flower to reach the nectar.

Nectar spur

INTERNAL ANATOMY
When sliced in half, the inside of this complex flower is revealed.

Two petals joined together act as a landing platform for bees

Front, or anterior, petal

Anthers and stigmas

Anthers and stigmas removed from flower

Anthers and stigmas

FROM FLOWER TO SEED
Bees are drawn to the flower by the brightly colored petals. Once the flower has been pollinated, the petals fall off. The female part of the flower then grows longer to form a five-sided capsule which contains the seeds. The seeds are shed when the fully grown capsule explodes.

Two petals joined together

Bee's-eye view of front of flower

Young seed capsule

Mature seed capsule

All sorts of flowers

Bear's-breeches

Mullein

Fireweed

Honeysuckle

Petals fuse
to form a
tu...

HOW MANY INDIVIDUAL FLOWERS are there on these two pages? The question is not quite as simple as it sounds. You would certainly need a magnifying glass to work out the answer, because the final figure adds up to at least 3,300. Some plants, such as the tulip, each have just a single flower. Others, like the dog rose, have a lot of flowers, but each one develops and blooms separately. Many other plants - including most of the plants on these two pages - produce flowers grouped together in clusters known as flower heads. Flower heads have many different shapes, and they vary widely in size and in the number of flowers they contain. The world's biggest individual flower, produced by the giant rafflesia (pp. 44-45), is completely dwarfed by the world's biggest flower head. This is grown by the rare South American puya, which reaches a height of nearly 33 ft (10 m).

Individual flower

Individual flower

Dog rose

Iris

REGULAR FLOWERS *above*
A flower is described as being regular if all the flower parts, including the sepals, petals, anthers, and stigma, are positioned on a simple circular plan, like the dog rose above.

The iris is a regular flower that can be cut symmetrically into three pieces.

The rose on this Tudor coin is based on the dog rose

FLOWER SPIRES *left*
Flowers in spires usually open in sequence, starting at the bottom. This sequence may take a number of weeks to complete. By the time the last flower has opened, the first may have already scattered seed.

IRREGULAR FLOWERS *right*
An irregular flower is still symmetrical (even), but in a more limited way. Most irregular flowers are bilaterally symmetrical, meaning that they can be divided into two halves that are mirror images of each other.

Sepal

Petal

Sweet pea

Clematis

SHOWY TEPALS
The sepals and petals of some flowers, like the clematis, are so similar that it is difficult to tell them apart. These parts are known as tepals (p. 16) and may be brightly colored.

Ray floret with single ray

Disk florets

Brightly colored tepal

NO PETALS?
The ray florets of composite flowers do not always have noticeable rays. Most species of chamomile have white rays (right), but in some varieties, although rays are present, they are difficult to see (left).

Eryngo

Eryngo has unusual domed flower heads

COMPOSITE FLOWERS
The flower heads of plants such as sunflowers and daisies are known as composite flowers, because they are composed of many tiny flowers clustered together. Sunflower heads have many hundreds of florets - disk florets in the center of the flower head, and ray florets, each with a single petal-like "ray," around the outer edge. In the yarrow (below), each flower head is made up of many individual disk florets. surrounded by about five ray florets. These flower heads are crowded together to form a bigger cluster with about 1,000 florets in all.

Sunflower

Ray florets

FLOWERS IN UMBELS
Not only are small flowers more visible if they are grouped together, but they also provide a better landing platform for pollinating insects. In plants of the carrot family, such as cow parsnip (right), flowers are grouped together in umbrella-shaped clusters called umbels. This family of plants is known as the umbellifers.

Flower head of cow parsnip

Flower head of cultivated yarrow

21

How a plant is pollinated

THE FASCINATING SHAPES and brilliant colors of many flowers have evolved over millions of years to make sure that tiny grains of pollen are carried from one plant to another. Pollen grains have to travel from the anthers to the stigma (pp. 16-17) for fertilization to occur and for seeds to be produced. Some plants are able to pollinate themselves (self-pollination), but most rely on receiving pollen from another plant of the same species (cross-pollination). Pollen may be scattered by wind or by water, but the most important pollinators are insects. Plants lure insects to their flowers with their bright colors and with food in the form of nectar. While the visiting insect feeds, pollen from the anthers is pressed on to its body, often at a particular place, such as on the back or on the head. The stigma of the flower that receives the pollen is in just the right place to collect it as the insect arrives. Some flowers are pollinated by a wide range of insects such as honeybees, bumblebees, hover flies, and butterflies. Others are more choosy and rely so heavily on a particular pollinato that no other insect species can do the job for them Some species of yucca, for example, are pollinated only by a small moth, called the yucca moth. In return, the yucca provides the moth with food and a home.

Pollen basket on hind leg

Honey guide

FAMILY HOM
Worker be bring nectar a pollen back the hive to fe the developi your

THE FLORAL FEEDING STATION
Honey guides (p. 12) on the flower guide the bee to the nectar. As the bees feed on the nectar, they also collect pollen in special baskets on their legs so it can be carried to the hive.

Bright yellow guide marks show bees where to land

Lower petal acts as landing platform

OPENING UP
The flower of the common toadflax is pollinated by bumblebees. When a visiting bee arrives, the throat of the flower is tightly closed. To reach the nectar at the back of the flower, the bee must open up the flower by pushing forward.

Nectar tube

CLIMBING IN
As the bumblebee climbs over the hump that seals the flower's throat and crawls inside in search of the nectar, it brushes against the anthers inside the top of the flower. These dust its back with pollen.

FEEDING TIM
As the bee feeds on the flower's necta any pollen it i already carrying is transferred from its back the stigma, ar the flower is pollinated.

The real thing!

Female impersonators

Some orchids use a clever trick to ensure that they are pollinated. Each flower looks and smells like a female fly, wasp, or bee. The impersonation is so convincing that the male tries to mate with the flower. When this happens, pollen sticks to the bee's body, and when the insect eventually flies off, the pollen is carried to the next flower.

...owers of the
...orchid

...ong proboscis

...ort
...oboscis

...RINKING STRAWS
...tterflies and moths suck
...nectar through the
...oboscis, which is
...llow like a drinking
...raw. The proboscis
...ay vary in
...ngth from a
...action of a
...illimeter to
...t (30 cm).
...hen
...e butterfly
...resting,
...e pro-
...oscis is
...iled up
...der the
...tterfly's
...ead.

POLLEN GRAINS
Although the largest pollen grains measure only about 0.2 mm across, they have very detailed shapes. When a pollen grain lands on the stigma of a plant of the same species, it grows a fine tube down the style (p. 17) until it reaches the female cell, or ovule.

Pollen grains magnified many times to show variety of shape.

BUTTERFLY POLLINATION
Butterflies are also important pollinators but, unlike bees, they do not feed on the pollen and so do not actively collect it. Instead, when they land on a flower to feed on the nectar, pollen from the anthers sticks to their bodies, ready to be carried to the next flower. Because butterflies have a highly developed sense of smell, butterfly-pollinated flowers are often scented. Many flower in late summer when butterflies are most abundant.

Proboscis sucks up nectar

Pollen from anthers sticks to butterfly's body

Wild marjoram

? >

Strange pollinators

Many flowers are pollinated by bees and butterflies (pp. 22-23), but some plant species depend on quite different creatures for pollination. Some are pollinated by the sort of flies that are attracted by the smell of decay. Others rely on birds, which are attracted to the flowers by bright colors and the sweet smell of nectar. Many plants are highly adapted for specific pollinators. The list of these species includes not only insects and birds, but also bats, mice, possums, and even slugs.

POLLINATION UNDERGROUN
Some orchids in Australia gro and flower underground, whe they live on the decaying remains of other plants. The picture on the left shows the flower of one of these species. These flowers are most probably pollinated by a soil-dwelling creature, although it is not yet known exactly which one.

Hairs on petals attract insects

Flowers are lilac at first, but turn red as they open

Pink bracts attract birds

Shiny surface

Cultivated fly-pollinated orchid

Flowers appear among bracts

A LURE FOR FLIES
Bees are attracted to flowers that have a sweet smell. Many flies, on the other hand, are attracted by the smell of decaying flesh. For thi reason, many flowe that rely on flies for pollination have a putrid odor. Some flowers, such as this orchid, have hairs o the surface of their petals to give them an animal-like feel. The shiny surface also attracts flies.

Urn plant

THE RED SIGNAL
Plants that are pollinated by birds often have red or pink petals or flower heads. Most birds have excellent color vision, and a bright red flower, which also produces nectar, readily attracts them. Because this urn plant lives high up on trees (p. 46), it needs to be noticeable to attract the attention of the bird pollinators. Most insects, apart from some butterflies, cannot see red, so it is an unusual color for insect-pollinated flowers.

Brushlike anthers

A BRUSH FOR BIRDS
Most species of hibiscus are pollinated by hummingbirds. A hummingbird hovers in front of the flower and inserts its long beak deep inside to reach the nectar. As it feeds, the anthers brush pollen onto its head, while the stigma, also brushing its head, collects pollen from another flower. The flower shown here is in an upright position. In its natural state it would normally be horizontal.

Hibiscus flower

BIZARRE BEAUTY
The yellow calla lily is pollinated by insects called fungus gnats. Its separate male and female flowers grow on a central spike, or spadix, and are enveloped by a bright yellow bract, called a spathe. The insects, carrying pollen from the male flowers of other plants, crawl to the base of the spathe, where they become trapped by downward-pointing hairs. As they move around, they pollinate the female flowers. The hairs then wither, and as the insects crawl out they are dusted with pollen from the mature male flowers and move on to the next plant.

Bright yellow spathe envelops flowers on spadix

Yellow calla lily

POSSUM POLLINATION
The Australian honey possum is a tiny animal that lives entirely on the pollen and nectar of flowers like this banksia. It collects its unusual food with its long snout and brushlike tongue. Apart from the possum, the only other mammals to pollinate flowers are rodents and bats.

"Window" cells let in light

Flies fall down this hollow tube and are trapped by downward-pointing hairs

Trapped flies try to escape by flying up toward the light and become covered with pollen

Landing flap

TAKING PRISONERS
This weirdly shaped flower is produced by a South American creeper. It lures flies by its smell of rotting fish. The flies enter the flower and are imprisoned within it overnight. When the flower begins to wither, the flies - now covered in pollen - can escape.

Colorful lobe attracts flies

Brazilian birthwort

From flower to fruit

AFTER A FLOWER HAS BEEN POLLINATED (pp. 22-23), it normal has to be fertilized before it will produce seeds and fruit When a pollen grain lands on the stigma of a flower of th same species, it germinates to produce a pollen tube. Th grows through the stigma and down the style to fertili the ovule (p. 17). One of the two male cells in the polle grain fuses with the egg cell in the ovule. This fuse cell then divides to form an embryo plant. food reserve, or endosperm, is forme around the embryo plant by the secon male cell, which fuses with two other cel in the ovule. The embryo plant, together wi its food store and protective coat, or testa, known as the seed. The fruit is usually forme from the ovary, the protective structure aroun the seeds. However, in some cases, other par of the flower protect both the seed and th ovary. In the rose, the "pips" inside th rose hip are technically the fruit and the fleshy outer part is know as the receptacle. The fru often helps in scattering see The most obvious fruits a sweet, juicy, and bright colored, tempting animals eat them and so scatter th seeds (p. 28). However, th fruits of some plants includ dry pods that flick th seeds in all directions (p. 29 or fluffy plumes that hel carry the seeds and frui high on the breeze (p. 30

WINTER FEAST
Fruits are an important source of winter food for many animals. Here a redwing feasts on fallen apples and may help to spread the apples' seeds.

Sepals protect developing bud

EARLY DAYS
Even before the rose comes into flower, the beginnings of the rose hip can be clearly seen. The top of the stem, to which the flower parts are attached, is round and swollen, as this bud shows. The female parts of the flower, the ovaries and ovules, are inside this swollen area, or receptacle.

Receptacle containing ovaries

THE ROSE IN BLOOM
As the bud opens, the flower gives off its sweet scent, which attracts bees for pollination (pp. 22-23). Once the flower has been pollinated and the ovules fertilized, the receptacle begins to swell.

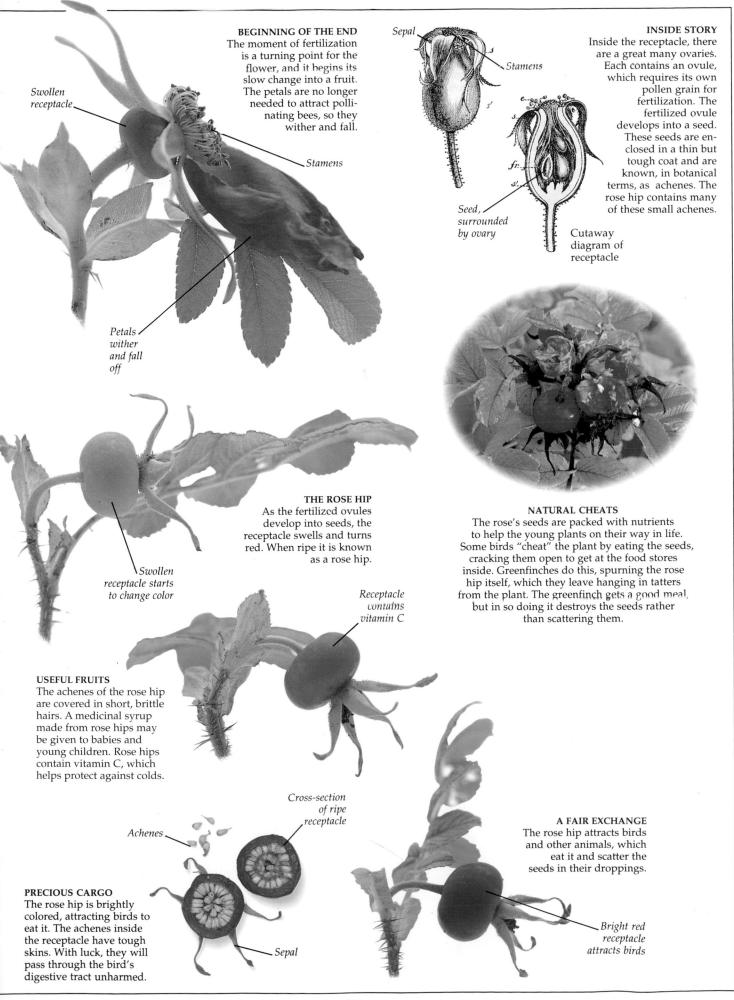

BEGINNING OF THE END
The moment of fertilization is a turning point for the flower, and it begins its slow change into a fruit. The petals are no longer needed to attract pollinating bees, so they wither and fall.

Swollen receptacle

Stamens

Petals wither and fall off

Sepal

Stamens

Seed, surrounded by ovary

INSIDE STORY
Inside the receptacle, there are a great many ovaries. Each contains an ovule, which requires its own pollen grain for fertilization. The fertilized ovule develops into a seed. These seeds are enclosed in a thin but tough coat and are known, in botanical terms, as achenes. The rose hip contains many of these small achenes.

Cutaway diagram of receptacle

THE ROSE HIP
As the fertilized ovules develop into seeds, the receptacle swells and turns red. When ripe it is known as a rose hip.

Swollen receptacle starts to change color

NATURAL CHEATS
The rose's seeds are packed with nutrients to help the young plants on their way in life. Some birds "cheat" the plant by eating the seeds, cracking them open to get at the food stores inside. Greenfinches do this, spurning the rose hip itself, which they leave hanging in tatters from the plant. The greenfinch gets a good meal, but in so doing it destroys the seeds rather than scattering them.

Receptacle contains vitamin C

USEFUL FRUITS
The achenes of the rose hip are covered in short, brittle hairs. A medicinal syrup made from rose hips may be given to babies and young children. Rose hips contain vitamin C, which helps protect against colds.

Cross-section of ripe receptacle

Achenes

A FAIR EXCHANGE
The rose hip attracts birds and other animals, which eat it and scatter the seeds in their droppings.

PRECIOUS CARGO
The rose hip is brightly colored, attracting birds to eat it. The achenes inside the receptacle have tough skins. With luck, they will pass through the bird's digestive tract unharmed.

Sepal

Bright red receptacle attracts birds

How seeds are spread

Agrimony

As ALL GARDENERS KNOW, a patch of bare soil never stays bare for long. Within days, seedlings start to spring up, and if the conditions are right, they eventually cover the ground. Even if the earth is sterilized by heating so that all the seeds are killed, more somehow arrive and germinate. Plants have evolved some very effective ways of spreading their seeds. In certain plants, exploding seed pods fling the seeds into the air. Others have flying or floating seeds, or fruits, which are carried far and wide by the wind and by water currents. Animals also play their part. Many plants have fruits with hooks that stick to fur. The seeds of some species develop inside tasty berries. The berries are eaten by animals and birds, and the seeds pass through these creatures unharmed and fall to the ground, where they germinate.

Fruits have hooks

Each fruit has many tiny hooks

Common burdock

Lotus seed heads

Seed held in cup

Dried lotus seed head from above

Lotuses growing in ancient Egypt

HITCHING A RIDE
The best way to find out which seeds are scattered by animals is to go for a walk through rough grassland. You will probably return home with the fruits of a number of different plants stuck to your clothes. Known as burs, these fruits have hooks and spines that cling to the fur and wool of passing animals. When the burs are rubbed or scratched off, their seeds fall to the ground and germinate.

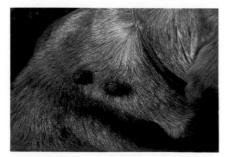

Burs cling to the fur on this dog's back

WASHED AWAY
The lotus is a water plant that produces its seeds in a flattened head. When the seeds are ripe, they fall onto the water's surface and float away. Lotus seeds can live for a very long time. Some have been known to germinate more than 200 years after they were shed.

Some plants scatter their seeds with natural catapults. These work by suddenly releasing tension that builds up as the seed case grows: the seed case splits open, flinging the seeds in all directions. These catapults are triggered in a number of ways. Some, particularly the pods of pea-family plants such as vetches, burst open when the sun dries them. Others, such as the Himalayan balsam (p. 18), are triggered by the movement of the wind or by an animal brushing against the plant.

Closed seed pod

When touched, the seed case curls up suddenly and the seeds are flicked out

exploded d pod

Seeds of meadow cranesbill are catapulted out

Himalayan balsam flower

Tiny, light seeds

Columbine

BLOWING IN THE WIND
Seeds that are scattered by the wind must be small and light if they are to be carried any distance by the breeze. When the wind shakes the seed heads of plants such as the opium poppy and columbine, the seeds travel just a short distance from the parent plant. When a thistle seed head catches the wind, its fruits (containing the seeds) can be swept high into the air and be carried much farther.

Seeds are sprinkled

Opium poppy

Fruits have parachutes so they can be carried by the wind

Pods of cow etch snap open hen dry

Intact pod

HUNNING THE LIGHT
e ivy-leaved toad-
x grows on walls
d rockfaces. As
seeds ripen, the
ems carrying the
ed heads grow
vay from the
ht, pushing the
eds into cracks
d crevices. This
sures that they
ve somewhere
itable to germinate.

Canadian thistle

Borne on the wind

ACCORDING TO TRADITION, if you make a wish and then blow on a dandelion's seed head, your wish will come true if all the seeds blow away in one puff. Whether or not the wish ever comes true, the custom certainly helps the plant to spread. The seeds of the dandelion are encased in tiny fruits and have their own special feathery parachutes to help them float through the air. If you blow on them, you may be starting the seeds on a journey that takes them high up and far away. The dandelion's flower, like that of the sunflower (p. 21), is actually a composite flower head made up of many tiny florets. Each of the florets produces a single fruit. Like the dandelion, many other composite plants, such as hawkweeds, rag-worts, and thistles, rely on the wind to scatter their seeds. The fruits of some of these have parachutes; others have fine hairs that stick out in all directions to form a feathery ball. Many of these plants are troublesome weeds because they quickly colonize bare soil in gardens and on farmland.

Dandelion's tiny fruits float away on the breeze

1 OPENING TIME
The dandelion's flower opens in the morning and closes in the afternoon or when it rains. The plant's name comes from the French *dent de lion,* meaning lion's tooth, which describes the jagged edges of the leaves.

Flower closes before seeds form

Flower head open, waiting to be pollinated by a passing insect

2 THE SEEDS START TO FORM
After opening and closing for a number of days, during which time it may be pollinated, the flower finally closes, and seed formation begins. Gradually the yellow petals wither away, and the "pappus," which is the name given to the small circle of hairs attached to the top of each fruit, starts to grow longer. This is the beginning of the parachute.

Bracts (specialized leaves) protect developing seed head

*Seed head
opens when
parachutes
are formed*

*Bracts
fold
back*

*Fully opened
seed head*

OPENING OUT
The seed head begins to open only
en the weather is dry. At first, the
achutes are squashed together, but
he bracts around the edge of the
d head fold back, the parachutes
;in to expand.

4 READY TO GO
If the air is still, the
fruits may spend several
days attached to the seed
head. This is a dangerous
time for them, because gold-
finches and other seed-eating
birds are likely to peck
them off and eat them.

*Parachutes attached
to tiny fruits*

5 LIFTOFF
A slight breeze is all that is
needed to lift the parachutes into the
air. They may fall nearby, but if there
is enough updraft they can be carried
for long distances. When a fruit lands,
it no longer needs the parachute that
has carried it on its journey, and this
breaks off. Over the winter the seed
sinks into the soil, waiting for the
spring when it will germinate.

Spreading without seeds

Piggyback plant

PLANTS CAN REPRODUCE in two quite different ways. As well as reproducing by means of seeds, they can sometimes also turn small pieces of themselves into new plants. This is known as vegetative reproduction. When a plant reproduces in this way, the young plantlets are genetically identical to the parent. This is quite different from reproduction with seeds, which produce seedlings that are all slightly different from their parents. Vegetative reproduction is very useful for farmers and gardeners. It means that they can multiply a plant that has attractive flowers or tasty fruit, knowing that each young plant will have exactly the characteristics they want. Some of the oldest plants in the world are reproduced by this process, like creosote plant "clones" in California. Each clone is created when a single creosote bush begins to spread by producing young plants connected to it. The original creosote bush at the center, which began life about 10,000 years ago, is now long dead, but its clones are still alive and spreading today.

THE PIGGYBACK PLANT
The piggyback plant has an unusual way of reproducing. Tiny new plantlets grow at the base of the older leaves and look as though they are having a piggyback ride.

Creepi crowfo

Parent plant

CREEPING STEMS
Some plants, such as the creeping crowfoot, spread by means of stolons, which are leafy stems that grow along the ground. When the stolons reach a certain length, a new, young plant develops from a bud at the leaf node (p. 9) and the stolon eventually withers away completely.

Fallen plantlets

Strawberry plant

Parent plant

Stolon, or runner

Bud at leaf node

Chandelier plant

PLANTLETS AT LEAF TIPS
Kalanchoes are succulents (p. 53), many of which reproduce by developing tiny plantlets along the edges of their leaves. Others, like this chandelier plant, have them just at the tips. When a plantlet is mature, it falls off the parent plant and takes root in the soil beneath.

STRAWBERRY RUNNERS
After they have fruited, strawberry plants produce long stolons known as runners which spread out over the ground. Strawberry growers wait until the young plants have rooted and then cut the runners. The new plants can be transplanted to make a new strawberry bed.

A MYTH EXPLODED
The famous tumbleweed of the western prairies is uprooted by strong winds after it has flowered and is often blown far away from the place where it grew. Because it is dead, the plant cannot put down roots once it comes to a halt, as is often supposed. Instead, it spreads by seeds. The plant scatters them as it tumbles along the ground.

Iris
rhizome

Tuber of
Jerusalem
artichoke

RHIZOMES

A rhizome is a usually horizontal stem produced by a perennial plant (p. 13), either underground or on the surface. As the rhizome spreads, it occasionally divides, producing roots, stems, and leaves. The oldest part of the rhizome may die away so that these new shoots form separate plants.

TUBERS

Tubers are swollen underground stems. They store food to produce new plants and also to help the parent plant survive in difficult conditions. When gardeners and farmers uproot tuber crops like potatoes, they have to be careful to dig up every one. If even part of the potato is left in the ground, it will sprout to produce a new plant the following spring.

Tuber of potato

olon

Young plant
forming at tip
of stolon

Young plant grows
from a bud at the
leaf node

Tulip bulb

BULBS

A bulb consists of a bud surrounded by short, very swollen leaves, with flattened underground stems. Some bulbs, such as the tulip, produce one or more new bulbs around its base every year. These can be broken off the parent bulb to form new plants.

unner

New bulbs
form around
the base of
the old bulb

AVES THAT TAKE ROOT

ants that live in dry
aces often have fleshy
aves that are full of
ater. If these leaves
e broken off, they can
rvive for a long time
cause they do not dry
t as quickly as normal,
n leaves. While
ey are lying on
e ground,
any of them
n put down
ots and de-
lop into
w plants.

Crassula nealana

BULBS ABOVE AND BELOW GROUND

This species of onion has both bulbs and bulbils, small bulblike structures that form above ground in place of flowers.

Bulbils may fall
to the ground
and take
root

Fleshy
leaves
can root
themselves

Bulb underground

Top of plant

Christmas-cheer

*Allium
paradoxum*

33

Living leaves

LEAVES ARE SO VARIED that botanists had to invent a whole new vocabulary to describe their shapes and the way they are fixed to plants. One reason for all this variety is that each species of plant has its own special problems in harvesting sunlight (pp. 14-15). A plant living on the gloomy floor of a rain forest, for example, may need large leaves to catch enough light. A plant growing on a cliff top has plenty of light but is lashed by strong winds. So it needs small, strong leaves if it is to survive. Some plants have more than one type of leaf. This is most marked in plants which start their lives underwater but then flower above it. One example of this is the water buttercup. Its submerged leaves are fine and feathery, to let water flow past without tearing them; its upper leaves are flat and broad so they can float on the surface.

Water plants often have feathery leaves to allow the water to flow past without damaging them

CHANGING COLOR
The leaves of herb Robert change from green to crimson as autumn approaches, or in very dry weather.

PARALLEL VEINS *left*
The leaves of plants such as grasses, orchids, and lilies have parallel veins (p. 9). These straplike leaves are from a member of the lily family.

FURRY LEAVES
Some leaves have "fur," which helps to reduce water loss. These leaves are from a chrysanthemum which was cultivated, or grown in a garden.

FACING THE WIND
Wild asparagus lives on windy coasts. Instead of true leaves it has feathery, green, leaflike stems, called cladodes, which are able to withstand gales. Large, fleshy leaves would be torn to pieces.

WATERSIDE GIANTS
Gunneras grow on river-banks in tropical forests, but are sometimes found beside water in warmer parts of temperate countries. Their leaves can be enormous - as much as 6 ft (2 m) in diameter.

Asparagus

Older leaves

Young leaves

Leaf supported by strong ribs

DIFFERE
SHA
This eucalyp
tree has lea
of two tota
different shap
The leaves of
young stem parts
round, like coi
and each one co
pletely encircles
branch. The lea
on the older pa
of the stems ha
stalks and
shaped l
short stra

Undersi
of a section
a gunnera le

Leaflet

Leaves that are made up of a number of individual leaflets are called compound leaves

SLASHED LEAVES
The Swiss cheese plant grows in tropical forests, clinging to trees for support. It probably gets its name from its unusual leaves. With all their slashes and perforations they look like some types of very holey Swiss cheese.

Leaves without leaflets are known as simple leaves

Slashes appear as the leaf grows older

Peltate leaves are circular, with the stalk inserted in the middle

Waxy upper surface

EVERGREEN LEAVES *left*
Evergreen plants do not lose their leaves in the winter, so their leaves need to be tough to survive several years in the wind, sun, and rain. Rhododendron leaves have a waxy upper surface to prevent them from drying out. Some species also have feltlike down on their undersides to hold moisture and ward off insects.

Jacob's coat

Lungwort

Some varieties have red undersides

Rhododendron leaves

Downy underside

MULTICOLORED LEAVES
Garden plants often have multicolored leaves. The lungwort gets its name from its spotty leaves which give it the appearance of a human lung. In times gone by, it was also used as a cure for lung diseases.

Self-defense

Plants cannot run away from their enemies in the same way as animals, so they have evolved special weapons and armor to protect themselves. The main enemies of most plants are the animals that feed on them. These range in size from tiny insects, which suck sap or chew their way through leaves, to large mammals, which eat entire plants. To keep the smallest enemies at bay, many plants have a mat of fine hairs on the surface of their leaves. Larger animals are deterred by means of special weaponry which includes spines, thorns, and stings.

As a final defense, many plants have chemicals in their cells which make them unpleasant to eat. Once an animal has tasted the plant, it is unlikely to want to repeat the experience.

*Thorns gro\
in pa*

*Hole through\
which ants\
enter\
thorn*

*Dried\
acacia\
twig*

Gall

Ant

ANTS ON GUAR
Some acacia trees rely on ants to keep aw\
browsing animals. In return for food and lodgi\
the ants ferociously attack any animal which tr\
to feed on the tree's leaves. The ants eat the swe\
tasting pith of the thorns and make them hollo\
They also feed from a row of nectaries at the base\
each leaf. The bullhorn acacia even produces lit\
knobs of protein and fat at the tip of each leafl\
which insures that the ants protect the whole le\

*Barbs along\
edge of leaf*

This nettle sting has been magnified many times to show the sharp tip

*Long,\
sharp\
spines*

*Small,\
fleshy\
leaves*

CHEMICAL WARFA
The stings of the nettle a\
like hypodermic needle\
The walls of the sting c\
are covered with a glas\
like substance calle\
silica (p. 7). When \
animal brushes past t\
nettle, the stings punctu\
its skin and release\
cocktail of chemica\
which causes a painf\
irritation. On futu\
encounters anima\
remember the sting ar\
avoid the nett\

RUNNING INTO TROUBLE
Screw pines are tropical plants that have tough, sword-shaped leaves. These have rows of vicious barbs, not only along their edges, but also along their midribs. The barbs point away from the plant, so any animal trying to get near it runs the risk of being impaled, as it pushes forward.

*Octopus\
tree*

*Barbs\
along\
midrib*

*Stinging\
nettle*

PROTECTED LEAVES
Plants that live in hot, dry climates need to defend themselves because their leaves are a tempting source of food and water for animals. Many of them, such as cacti, do this with spines (pp. 52-53). This plant from Madagascar has spines that are longer than its leaves, making it very hard for large animals to reach them.

*Leaf of\
screw pine*

TANGLED
IN A TRAP

Thorns on flexible stems snag passing animals and give them a painful lesson, teaching them not to get too close again. Thorns can either be straight, as on this rose, or they can be curved, which makes them dig in when they are pulled. Some plants have thorns pointing in both directions along their stems. If an animal gets tangled in the plant, the thorns catch no matter which way it pulls.

Thistle
in flower

Woolly
thistle

ARMORED FLOWERS

Thistles are extremely successful plants, partly because they have an effective seed-scattering system (pp. 28–29) and partly because they are very well defended. Most thistles have spines on their stems as well as on their leaves. They also have spiny flaps, known as bracts, which protect their developing flower heads. The spines keep most animals away, although they do not deter sap-sucking insects such as aphids, which often feed in large numbers on thistles.

rs of straight
ns keep
nals away

*Spiny bracts protect
the developing
flower head*

ATH BY DROWNING
rs of leaves on the
m of the teasel meet
form little cups which
with water after
n. Each cup acts like
noat to protect the
nt. Snails and insects
to climb the plant to
d on its young leaves
t, faced with the
ter, they either turn
k or fall into the
at and drown.

*Young, spiny
flower head*

Holly
leaves

*Insects drowned in moat
formed at the point
where the paired
leaves meet*

Teasel

*Spines
protect
stem*

EXTRA WEAPONRY

Holly leaves are not only very leathery, they also have tough spines all around their edges. Compared to the leaves of deciduous trees, which lose their leaves every autumn, holly suffers very little from animal attack. These leaves are from a variety of holly which has been cultivated to produce extra spines. On holly trees, the lowest leaves are usually the spiniest. Those nearest the top may have no spines at all, as they are in less danger of being eaten.

Creepers and climbers

WHEREVER THERE IS MOISTURE AND WARMTH, plants struggle against each other for light. The tallest plant usually gets the greatest share, but it also has to spend the most energy in growing a strong stem, or a tree trunk, to hold up its leaves. But there are some plants - epiphytes (pp. 46-47) and climbers - which take a shortcut to the top. They take advantage of other plants and even buildings to get a place in the light with much less effort. Epiphytes may grow on the trunks or upper branches of trees and are lifted up with them as they grow. These plants do not have roots on the ground and are able to absorb all the water they need from the air and rainwater. Climbers need supports. Some twine themselves around a plant; others put out touch-sensitive feelers, or tendrils, which curl around the support when they come into contact with it. A third group of climbers raise themselves by means of stiff side branches, prickles, roots, or hairs.

GROWING IN A SPIRAL
Plants which grow in a spiral twist a set direction. Scarlet runner plants always twist in a clockwise directio a detail noticed by the artist who made this 16th-century woodcut of bean plant climbing up a stick.

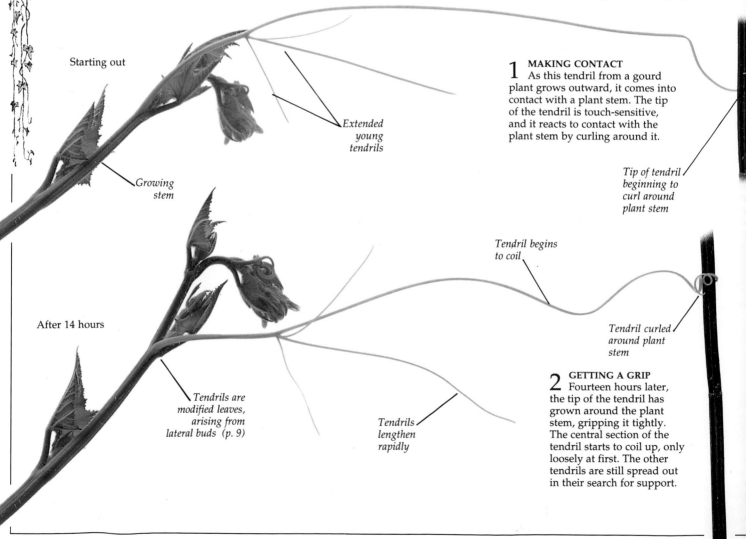

Starting out

Extended young tendrils

Growing stem

After 14 hours

Tendrils are modified leaves, arising from lateral buds (p. 9)

Tendrils lengthen rapidly

1 MAKING CONTACT
As this tendril from a gourd plant grows outward, it comes into contact with a plant stem. The tip of the tendril is touch-sensitive, and it reacts to contact with the plant stem by curling around it.

Tip of tendril beginning to curl around plant stem

Tendril begins to coil

Tendril curled around plant stem

2 GETTING A GRIP
Fourteen hours later, the tip of the tendril has grown around the plant stem, gripping it tightly. The central section of the tendril starts to coil up, only loosely at first. The other tendrils are still spread out in their search for support.

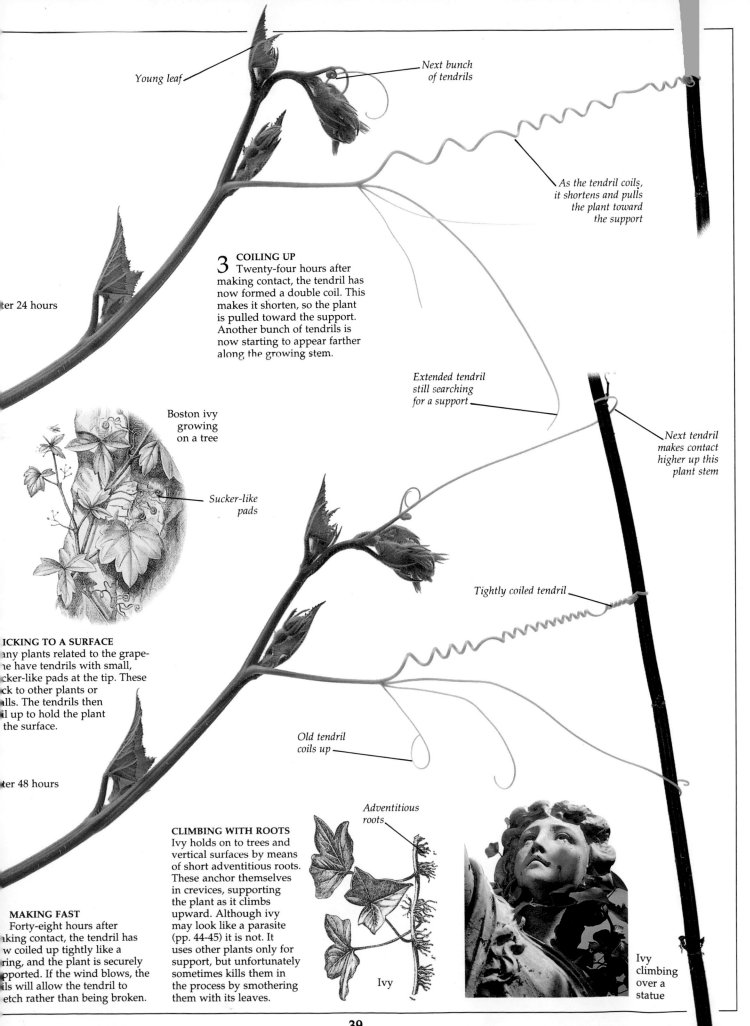

Young leaf

Next bunch of tendrils

As the tendril coils, it shortens and pulls the plant toward the support

3 COILING UP
Twenty-four hours after making contact, the tendril has now formed a double coil. This makes it shorten, so the plant is pulled toward the support. Another bunch of tendrils is now starting to appear farther along the growing stem.

...ter 24 hours

Extended tendril still searching for a support

Next tendril makes contact higher up this plant stem

Boston ivy growing on a tree

Sucker-like pads

Tightly coiled tendril

...ICKING TO A SURFACE
...any plants related to the grape-
...e have tendrils with small,
...cker-like pads at the tip. These
...ck to other plants or
...lls. The tendrils then
...l up to hold the plant
...the surface.

Old tendril coils up

...ter 48 hours

Adventitious roots

CLIMBING WITH ROOTS
Ivy holds on to trees and vertical surfaces by means of short adventitious roots. These anchor themselves in crevices, supporting the plant as it climbs upward. Although ivy may look like a parasite (pp. 44-45) it is not. It uses other plants only for support, but unfortunately sometimes kills them in the process by smothering them with its leaves.

Ivy

Ivy climbing over a statue

MAKING FAST
Forty-eight hours after
...aking contact, the tendril has
...w coiled up tightly like a
...ring, and the plant is securely
...pported. If the wind blows, the
...ls will allow the tendril to
...etch rather than being broken.

Meat eaters

ALTHOUGH MAN-EATING PLANTS belong to the world of fiction, there are many plants that eat insects and other small animals. These meat-eating or carnivorous plants fall into two groups. Some species, such as the Venus flytrap (pp. 42-43), have active traps with moving parts that catch their prey. Other species have inactive traps with no moving parts. They simply attract their victims with a scent like that of food, and then catch them on a sticky surface or drown them in a pool of fluid. The victims of carnivorous plants are mostly insects. Once an insect has been caught, it is slowly dissolved by the plant's digestive fluids. After many days, all that is left is the insect's exoskeleton - the hard outer casing of the body. The rest of the insect has been absorbed by the plant. Carnivorous plants can make food from sunlight like ordinary plants. The insects they catch are simply used as a dietary supplement - they are the plants' equivalent of vitamin tablets. Many plants need this extra source of food because they grow in waterlogged ground, where the soil doesn't have many nitrates and other essential nutrients.

SPECIALIZED LEAVES
All the animal traps shown on these two pages are modified leaves. The leaves of the Portuguese sundew are so sticky that they used to be hung up indoors to catch flies.

Flower of Cape sundew

Lid kee out ra

Rim

FATAL ATTRACTION
This colorful nepenthes pitcher lures passing insects.

Water flea trapped by a bladderwort

UNDERWATER TRAPS
Bladderworts are water plants that develop traps, in the form of tiny bladders, on their feathery leaves. If a small water animal swims past, the bubble-like bladder snaps open, and the animal is sucked inside.

THE STICKY SUNDEWS
The leaves of sundews are covered in hairs that produce droplets of sticky "glue." When an insect lands on one of the leaves, it sticks to the hairs, which then fold over and trap it.

Magnification of a fly trapped by hairs on sundew leaf

Cape sundew

LYING IN WAIT
Butterworts have circles of flat, sticky leaves. These plants may not look very threatening, but when an insect lands on a leaf, it becomes glued to the surface and eventually dies. The edges of the leaf very gradually curl inward, and the insect is digested. There are about 50 species of butterwort, most of which grow in marshy places.

Leaf covered with short, sticky hairs

Butterwo

Leaf of hanging pitcher plant

An 18th-century engraving
of hanging nepenthes
pitcher plants

DEATH IN THE SWAMPS
American pitcher plants catch
their food in the same way as the
hanging pitcher plants, but instead of
hanging from leaves, their pitchers grow up
from the ground. The inside of each pitcher
is lined with scales of wax, so the insects
are unable to hang on to the sides as they
tumble toward the liquid below. Once in
the liquid, the scales prevent them from
climbing back up the sides of
the pitcher.

*American pitcher
plant has a
frilly rim*

COBRA LILY *below*
The California pitcher
plant, or cobra lily,
looks like a snake rearing
up and flicking out its tongue.
Insects, lured by nectar,
enter the plant through the
"mouth." Once inside the pitcher,
they are confused by light shining
down through small "windows" at
the top. In the attempt to escape, the
insects fly continually toward the light,
but eventually become exhausted, drop
into the liquid, and drown.

*Rim where nectar
is produced*

"Windows"

ANGING PITCHER PLANT
e traps of hanging pitcher
ants grow at the ends of their
ves. Each one is like a jug and
s a lid to keep out the rain.
sects are lured to the pitcher
its bright color and by nectar
nich is produced around the
m. The surface of the rim is
ppery, so when insects try
settle on it, they lose their
oting, fall inside, and drown
the fluid at the bottom.
anging pitcher plants
ow in Southeast Asia.
e largest pitchers are
to 14 in (35 cm) deep
d hold a cupful
fluid.

*These insects are
being slowly
digested in the
fluid that collects
at the bottom of
the pitcher*

*Entrance to
pitcher
("mouth")*

Vertical cross-section
through hanging pitcher

This American
pitcher plant is
known as a parrot
pitcher plant

Cobra lily

Caught in a trap

To an unwary insect, the unusual leaf tips of the Venus flytrap appear most inviting. Not only is the insect attracted by what looks like a safe landing place, it is also tempted by the promise of food in the form of nectar. But it is all a trick. As soon as the insect settles, the leaf tips spring to life with lightning speed. Within a second, the hapless insect finds itself trapped as the two halves of the leaf snap shut. There is a second, slower phase of closing after the plant has tested what it has caught using sensory glands on the surface of its lobes. If the prey contains protein, the trap closes fully, and digestion begins. The traps of the Venus flytrap are formed by two kidney-shaped lobes at the tip of the leaf, with a hinge formed by the midrib. The entire leaf is green and therefore able to photosynthesize (pp. 14-15). Large bristles on the upper surface of the trap work like triggers with a clever device. If just one bristle is touched, by a raindrop for example, the trap stays open. But if two or more bristles are touched one after the other, it quickly shuts to catch its victim.

A MOST HORRIBLE TORTURE
Insects were not the only ones to be condemned to a frightful and lingering death, as this rather gruesome engraving shows.

Marginal teeth

Trigger bristle

Damselfly touches trigger bristles

Damselfly is caught in closing trap

Midrib of leaf

Kidney-shaped leaf tip

Lower part of leaf

Open trap

1 THE TRAP IS TRIGGERED
A damselfly lands on the trap and touches the trigger bristles on the trap's upper surface. Initially, special cells in the hinge, called motor cells, are filled with liquid. As soon as the triggers are fired, this liquid rushes out of the motor cells, making them collapse. This causes the trap to spring shut. The damselfly either does not notice this movement, or reacts too slowly.

2 CLOSING UP
After about one fifth of a second, the sides of the trap are already closing over their victim. Because the teeth on the edge point slightly outward, they help to make sure that the insect does not fall out as the trap shuts. Even if it has sensed danger, it is now too late for the damselfly to make its escape.

After one fifth of a second

An early
[19th]-century
[pai]nting of
[the] Venus
[flyt]rap by
[R]oute, who
[pai]nted the
[plan]ts kept by
[the] Empress
[Jos]ephine at
[Mal]maison
[(18]61)

Flower stem

GROWING A FLYTRAP

The first living specimen of the Venus flytrap arrived in England from America in the mid-18th century. Never before had such an unusual and spectacular plant been seen live in Europe, and it aroused great curiosity among botanists. Today Venus flytraps can be grown as potted plants. Because they come from waterlogged bogs with slightly acid soil, they must never be allowed to dry out and are best planted in peat. It is important to water them with distilled water, because tap water often contains dissolved minerals that will reduce the plant's chances of survival. Venus flytraps do produce clusters of white flowers, but this does not often happen with indoor specimens, especially if they are frequently fed with insects.

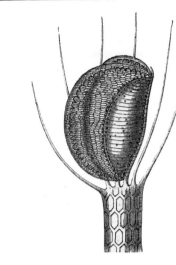

A WATERY HABITAT

Venus flytraps come from the bogs of North Carolina. Each plant grows from a small rhizome and produces several traps. Each trap can catch about three insects before it withers.

FLOATING TRAPS

This waterwheel plant is a small water plant that belongs to the same family of plants as the Venus flytrap and the sundews. Its leaves end in small traps that catch tiny water animals. They can close in one fiftieth of a second.

Marginal teeth closing around insect

Teeth on edge form a cage around the damselfly

Trap almost closed

3 COMING TOGETHER

After two fifths of a second, the teeth have almost met. They are arranged alternately, so that they do not crash into each other as the trap closes. Meanwhile, inside the trap, the trigger bristles fold back. This insures that they are not damaged and will be able to work again when the trap reopens.

4 ALL EXITS SEALED

When the trap shuts, its sides remain at a slight angle to each other. At this stage very small insects can climb out between the teeth, but the damselfly is too big and is securely held in. The trap would be wasted on small insects, as it can only digest two or three insects before it becomes ineffective. After 30 minutes the sides of the trap will close fully and the plant will begin to digest its prisoner.

5 DIGESTION

Special glands inside the trap secrete acid and substances called enzymes which will slowly digest all the soft parts of the insect's body. These glands later absorb the digested insect. It will take about two weeks for the damselfly to be fully digested, and for the trap to be ready for another meal. When the trap re-opens, the insect's hard exoskeleton, which includes the wings, will blow away.

[Af]ter two fifths
[of] a second

Parasitic plants

Giant rafflesia flower

PARASITIC PLANTS are cheats. Rather than making their own food using the energy from sunlight, they have developed a means of stealing the food made by other plants, known as host plants. Because they do not need sunlight, many parasitic plants spend most of their lives hidden from sight. They attach themselves to the stems or roots of their host plants by means of haustoria, or suckers. The haustoria penetrate the host's food channels and absorb the sugars and minerals which the parasitic plant needs to live. The world of parasitic plants is a complicated one. Some plants, such as mistletoe and eyebright, are only partly parasitic and are known as semiparasites. These plants have green leaves and can use the sun's energy to make some food themselves.

OLD TRADITION
The custom of kissing under the mistletoe may be older than you might think, for this plant was sacred to the Druids of ancient Britain.

Giant sepals unfold as flower opens

THE STINKING GIANT
The world's heaviest flower is a species of rafflesia, a parasite that lives on the roots of vines in the jungles of Southeast Asia. Each flower weighs nearly 15 lb (7 kg) and reaches up to 3 ft (1 m) in diameter. The flower fills the air with a putrid smell which attracts pollinating flies. This plant is the largest of 50 species, all of them completely parasitic.

Sepals are thick and fleshy

MAKING A BREAK-IN
Dodder stems spread over their hosts looking like lengths of tangled string. These stems develop haustoria which penetrate their host's food channels. Young dodders have roots to help them become established, but as they grow, the roots wither away.

Dodder flowers

Dodder stem twisting around stem of host plant

Dodder flowers   Haustoria penetrating stem of host

Plant passengers

NOT ALL PLANTS that live on others are parasites (pp. 44-45). In fact, many more of them are simply passengers that grow on larger plants, such as trees, without causing them any harm. Such plants are described as "epiphytic," and many of them can get all the water they need simply by absorbing it from the air or by collecting it in structures formed for the purpose. They collect minerals by removing them from trickling rainwater and plant debris. Being an epiphyte gives a small plant a chance to absorb a lot of light without the need of tall stems. So successful is this way of life that few trees are without their passengers. In cool parts of the world, epiphytes are usually small, simple plants, such as algae, lichens, and mosses. But in moist regions close to the equator, they are much larger. As well as the plants that spend their entire lives up in the trees, there are others that start or end their lives in this way. Some creeping plants, known as stranglers, germinate on trees and then become rooted in the soil. Others climb up onto plants but then their roots wither away, leaving them perched high up near the light.

These large, woody climbers, known as lianas, grow in tropical rain forests

Leaves have a special coating to reduce water loss

In the forests of Sri Lanka, epiphytic orchids grow on the trees

THE BROMELIAD'S PRIVATE POND
The bromeliads are a family of plants which includes the pineapple. Many of them grow on other plants. Instead of collecting water with long, aerial roots like orchids, they channel rainwater into a central reservoir (right) with their stiff, spiky leaves. Hairs on the leaves then absorb the water so the plant can use it. A big bromeliad holds over 1 gallon (5 liters) of water, and provides a home for water animals such as tree-frog tadpoles.

A species of
moth orchid

EPIPHYTIC ORCHIDS
There are about 18,000 species of orchid in
the world. Many tropical orchids live by
perching on other plants. Orchid seeds are
tiny, and a single plant may produce a
million of them. The wind blows the seeds
of epiphytic species onto the bark of trees,
where they can germinate. Each of these
perching orchids has three types of aerial
root, for clinging to the host, for absorbing
minerals, and for taking water from the
atmosphere. Some epiphytic orchids store
water and food reserves in swollen stems
called pseudobulbs.

*Flowers produce
wind-scattered seeds*

*Thick, trailing
aerial roots
collect moisture
as well as
minerals from
trickling
rainwater*

Liana stems
make a
natural rope

NATURAL ROPES
Lianas are climbing plants with flexible woody stems. Sometimes they
twine around each other for mutual
support. If the original support dies
and decays, the lianas are left sus-
pended from the forest canopy. Other
plants, called stranglers, start life
above ground and then grow roots
downward. Their roots form a mesh
around the trunks of trees and eventually kill the support.

Tarzan used lianas to swing from
tree to tree across the jungle

Adapting to water

THE FIRST PLANTS ON EARTH evolved in water. Today water still teems with microscopic plants that have changed little from those distant ancestors. But aquatic flowering plants have a different history. Their ancestors originally left water and evolved on land, but as time went by they returned to a watery habitat. Only a few flowering plants, such as the eelgrasses, live in the sea. Far more plant species live in freshwater ponds, lakes, and rivers. Most of them are rooted to the bottom, but some have no roots and receive all the nutrients they need from the water instead of the soil. Some water plants are not often noticed because they spend all their lives underwater. Species like the water lily are easier to spot because their leaves float on the surface. Plants such as reeds and rushes form a group known as emergent plants. They grow up out of the water and often form thick beds at the water's edge.

Glossy yellow flowers

LEAVIN[G] THE WAT[ER]
The grea[t] spearwort is [an] example of an em[er]gent water pla[nt]. It starts its annu[al] cycle of grow[th] underwater b[ut] quickly reach[es] the surface. T[he] flowers bloom abo[ut] 2 ft (60 cm) abo[ve] the water, whe[re] they attra[ct] pollinating inse[cts].

Greater spearwort

Spear-shaped leaves

HISTORIC HIDEOUT
The pharaoh's daughter discovers Moses hidden in the bulrushes at the water's edge.

UNDERWATER LEAVES
Fanwort has finely divided underwater leaves which are not damaged by the current.

Fanwort

19th-century
engraving of
papyrus growing
by the Nile
in Egypt

FLOATING ON THE SURFACE
When young, the leaves of water lilies are
rolled up underwater like short tubes. In spring,
the leaves reach the surface, where they open
out and lie flat to form pads. In some ponds
and lakes, water lilies and other plants with
floating leaves can completely cover the
water's surface, robbing submerged plants of
the light they need to survive. The
leaves are tough and leathery so
water easily runs off their surface.

*Tough, waxy
surface
repels water*

LANT FOR PAPER
yrus is a giant reed that grows up to
t (3 m) high. The Ancient Egyptians
iscovered that the pith in the middle
of its stems could be used to make
a material for writing on – the
very first paper.

*Flexible stalks attach
leaves to the roots,
which are anchored
in the muddy bottom*

AZONIAN GIANT
e floating leaves of the
azonian water lily can
ch a diameter of more
n 6 ft (2 m).

Surviving above the snowline

THE HIGHER THE ALTITUDE at which a plant grows, the colder the temperatures it has to endure. Very low temperatures create specific problems for plant life. Thin mountain air holds little heat, and on exposed mountainsides, high winds create a chill factor which makes the cold even more penetrating. In addition, low rainfall and thin, frozen soils mean that water is scarce. However, many plants manage to survive despite the harsh conditions. In the Himalayas, flowering plants have been found at over 20,000 ft (6,000 m), sheltering in hollows in the frost-shattered rock. These plants, known as alpine plants, are generally small and compact so they can survive on the high mountain peaks or in the frozen polar regions. Alpine plants often grow in dense cushions or flattened mats, giving them protection against the cold, drying wind. Upright, spreading branches would quickly be battered by the wind, and large leaves would lose valuable heat and water.

An unsteady perch for a determined alpine plant collector

Mountain avens

Mountain kidney vetch

QUICK WORK
When spring comes, the mountain slopes burst into color as alpine plants begin to flower. In high mountain areas where the summers are short, these plants have to flower and produce seeds quickly before winter comes around again.

HAIRY LEAVES
Mountain avens are plants that grow on high ground, from the Alps to the Arctic. Fine hairs on the undersides of their leaves keep them from losing too much water and act as insulation.

BUILT IN SUNSCREENS
This mountain kidney vetch grows high in the Alps and has leaves covered in hairs. Like those of the silversword, the hairs protect the leaves from sun damage, reduce water loss, and act as insulation.

RADIATION HAZARD
The sunlight that falls on high mountaintops in the tropics is more intense than anywhere else on Earth. The silversword grows in Hawaii at altitudes of up to 13,000 ft (4,000 m). Its leaves are covered with fine white hairs which protect the plant from much of the sun's dangerous ultraviolet radiation.

PLANT CUSHIONS
This dwarf hebe from New Zealand is an evergreen plant with small tough leaves that can withstand sharp frost. It grows in dense cushions which· trap heat, prevent wind damage, and reduce water loss. These cushions are covered in white flowers every spring.

Dwarf hebe

Garland
flower

Mazus
reptans

AT
AINST
E GROUND
ny alpine plants
ead over the ground
he form of flat
ts, keeping out of
path of icy winds.
is "prostrate" or
t-forming plant,
zus reptans, is from
Himalayas.

A MINIATURE SHRUB
This alpine daphne, or
garland flower, is a shrub
in miniature. Larger
daphnes grow at lower levels.

SMALL LEAVES
Moltkias are members
of the forget-me-not
family. Unlike many
of their lowland
relatives, alpine
moltkias have small
leaves which are
better able to with-
stand high winds.

MOUNDS OF COLOR
Like many alpine plants, this beautiful
phlox from North America has brilliantly
colored flowers. They stand out against the
rocky slopes and attract pollinating insects.

Alpine
phlox

Hoary rockrose

AL PROTECTION
untain rockroses
protected from the
ather in two ways. The
shy plants are able to
nd up to strong wind
ter than those with
er, more rigid stems,
d their leaves and stems
covered with fine
irs which act as
sulation at night.

TWO WAYS TO SPREAD
This species of storksbill
lives in the high Pyrenees.
It spreads both by seeds
and by its creeping
root system (p. 32).

MOUNTAIN DWARF
Many mountain plants
which survive at
great heights, like
this St.-John's-wort, are
much smaller than their
lowland relatives.

St.-John's-
wort

Storksbill

51

Living without water

No PLANT CAN LIVE entirely without water, but in very dry regions, where water is scarce, some plants, called succulents, are able to survive for a number of years between rainstorms. In the world's driest places, rain often comes in irregular but heavy bursts, so the plants that live there have evolved ways of collecting as much water as possible during downpours. The water is then stored in preparation for the next drought. Many succulents have very long roots, most of which grow near the surface, so that when it rains, they can collect water from a wide area. Once the water is inside the plant, it is kept there by a number of special adaptations. Plants normally lose water from stomata, tiny pores in the leaf surface. The plant can control these pores and keeps them closed if it begins to lose too much water. Many succulents open the pores only at night, when the air is cool and less water can evaporate. Some of these plants have got around the problem of water loss by losing their leaves altogether.

Mammillaria elongata

Ferocactus

Echinocere

Fake flowers stuck on by a clever florist to enhance the plant's appearance

Cross-section of square stem

Row of spines

Clusters of spines

Big-toothed euphorbia

Prickly pear cactus

SIMILAR SHAPES FOR SIMILAR LIFESTYLES
Not all the spiny plants that live in dry places are cacti. The cactus-like plant on the far left is actually a spurge, a plant quite unrelated to the two cacti to its right. Like the cacti, it has lost its leaves and developed a tough, water-holding stem. This is a typical example of "convergent evolution," in which plants or animals in similar environments evolve in similar ways.

THE CACT
FAM
Almost all true ca come from the Americ Because they live in ve dry places, they have h to evolve strange shapes be able to survive. Most ca have very thick stems a thick groups of spines inste of normal leaves. Th spines may protect the pla from heat and cold as well from attack by animals. Ma cacti have ridges down th stems to allow them expand and store wa when it rai

Cleistocactus

Cross-section of round stem

THE GIANT SAGUARO
The saguaro is one of the world's tallest cacti. A 250-year-old plant can be 50 ft (15 m) high and can weigh 6 tons.

ucculents

ants with fleshy leaves or stems for storing water are own as succulents and include the group of plants called cti. There are three main types of succulent. Stem succu-nts, such as cacti, store water in their stems and tend live in the driest climates. Leaf succulents, some of nich are shown on this page, store water in their aves and grow in damper conditions. Finally, ot succulents have thickened roots which rve as water reservoirs.

The leaves of this species of *Cotyledon* are fleshy, with a waxy surface, to reduce water loss.

Blue echeveria

The whitish "bloom" on the surface of the leaves of the window plant protects the plant from the harsh rays of the sun.

AF SUCCULENTS
af succulent plants live in ni-desert and also in salt rshes, where the salty nditions mean that fresh ter has to be carefully nserved. In prolonged dry ather their leaves inkle up. When it rains, e leaves swell as the nt takes in water.

The plump leaves of Haworthia cymbiformis *arc swollen with stored water.*

Blue echeveria

Haworthia cymbiformis

Panda plant

The necklace vine gets its name from its leaves, which look as if they have been threaded on a string.

Panda plant

indow plant

Cotyledon

Necklace vine

FLEETING FLOWERS
Many desert plants are "ephemerals." This means that they germinate only after rain, and then com-plete their life cycle very rapid-ly. For a few days after rain, the desert is ablaze with their flowers. This sea of little yellow flowers is made up of thousands of desert sunflowers, which have all come into bloom at once in the Utah desert.

AVES THAT WITHSTAND DROUGHT
s much as nine tenths of the weight of a succulent f may be stored water. To conserve this vital store, e leaves have a waxy surface which cuts down tran-iration, the process by which leaves lose water. me succulent leaves have a woolly surface which lps to keep the leaf cool, reducing water loss. cculent leaves have evolved in many unrelated nt species throughout the dry regions of the world.

Food from plants

PLANTS HAVE BEEN CULTIVATED as food crops for thousands of years. The earliest humans lived in nomadic groups, roaming the countryside in search of food. Eventually these peoples settled down, and instead of collecting plant foods from the wild they began to cultivate them. When the time came to gather seeds to produce crops for the following year, they tended to take seeds from the healthiest plants. As they did this year after year, they began to produce better crop plants. Later, more deliberate efforts were made to improve crops by selecting and cultivating the strongest plants, and this process is continuing today. As farming settlements were established independently in different parts of the world, so different crops were cultivated in each place. This meant that when early travelers first visited distant continents, they found many new and exciting foods to bring home. The crops we eat today come from many different parts of the world.

MARKET IN PERU
Potatoes originated in the high Andes of South America. Many varieties of potato are still grown there, as this market scene shows.

KEPT IN THE DARK
If allowed to grow in the light, chicory has a bitter taste. To reduce this bitterness, the plant is cut back to the ground and then allowed to regrow with almost no light. The pale, "blanched" leaves of the new chicory shoot are far less bitter. If cultivated chicory were grown entirely in the light, the plant would look very similar to its ancestor.

Primitive form of corn plant and cob

Blanched shoot of cultivated chicory

Modern corncob

Wild chicory

PRIMITIVE CORN
Corn is a cereal; like wheat and rice it is a member of the grass family. It was first cultivated in Central America, and some primitive forms of corn can still be found growing there. As a result of selective breeding, the size and shape of the modern corncob have been increased.

Fruits of a wild tomato, from Mexico

Wild cabbage has dark green, leathery leaves

LEAVING THE PAST BEHIND

The wild cabbage grows near the sea. It has leathery leaves, loosely arranged on a branched stem. Years of breeding have got rid of the plant's bitter taste and made its leaves more juicy. The shape of the plant has also changed so that, in most cultivated cabbages, the leaves are packed tightly together. In the "red" varieties of cabbage, certain natural pigments have been built up as a result of selective breeding.

Flowers of wild tomato; flowers of cultivated tomato are very similar.

Beefsteak tomato

...ltivated tomatoes ...ve become ...ch bigger ...ough ...eding.

BIGGER - AND BETTER?

The tomato's wild ancestor is a red berry the size of a small grape. It is much sweeter than the modern tomato, and more strongly flavored.

...OWING IN WATER

...e, which was cultivated in the Far ...st at least 5,000 years ago, forms the ...ple cereal diet of over one half of the ...rld's population. It usually grows in ...ds of standing water, known ...paddies

Flower head of wild carrot

Working in the paddies

Modern cabbage

Wild carrot root

Cultivated carrot

Modern red cabbage

...IBLE ROOTS

...e wild carrot is found all over ...rope and through much of Asia, ...t its roots are white or only ...ghtly colored. Only in Afghan-...an is there a variety of wild ...rot with orange roots. The ...rot was probably first cultivated ...that region and then introduced ...other parts of the world.

CARROTS AND CABBAGES

This detail from a 16th-century painting by the Dutch artist Lucas Van Valkenborch proves that even 400 years ago there was a wide variety of vegetables available.

The story of wheat

WHEAT HAS BEEN CULTIVATED by humans as a valuable source of food for at least 9,000 years. Grains of wheat have been found preserved in ancient Egyptian tombs, and it is known that it was the chief cereal of the ancient Greeks and Romans. The cultivation of wheat originated in the region known as the Fertile Crescent, which includes part of Israel, Turkey, Iraq, and Iran. Once a rich farming area, today much of it is desert. Wheat is now grown in most parts of the world and the quality has improved greatly. The early, primitive species, such as einkorn and emmer, had long thin stalks which were easily broken in bad weather. The small grains meant that a large number of plants only produced a relatively low yield of grain. Today, as a result of extensive breeding programs, better varieties have been found which have higher yields, resist drought, and withstand disease.

FOOD FOR THE MASSES
People have grown cereals for food for thousands of years, as this picture from the 11th century shows.

CUTTING THE CORN
Wild grasses drop their ripe seeds. The first farmers selected plants that held on to the seeds, so that the grain could be harvested.

Grains of wild einkorn

Grains of emmer

WILD EINKORN
This wild grass is probably one of the ancestors of all cultivated wheats. It has long, thin stalks and small heads and grains.

EINKORN
This early wheat species is still grown in parts of Turkey for animal feed. Its grains are small and difficult to thresh.

WILD WHEAT
This wild grass is the ancestor of emmer, another primitive wheat. The heads and grains are larger than those of einkorn.

EMMER
Emmer was the chief cereal in ancient Greek and Roman times. It is one of the ancestors of modern cultivated wheats.

long, spiky
stles attached
scales around
h grain are
ed awns

Spelt grains

WHEATFIELD PRAIRIE
Today's wheat is much shorter than that of a century ago. Breeders have reduced the amount of stalk, so that the plant does not bend over; a curved stalk makes it difficult to harvest the grain. This is an important step forward for the major grain-producing countries of the world, where vast areas of wheat are grown.

Brown bread
baked with
unbleached
whole-wheat
flour

SPELT
The great leap forward for wheats came when emmer crossed, or hybridized, with wild goat grass that was growing as a weed in wheat fields. The result was spelt wheat, which is still cultivated in parts of northwest Europe.

Durum wheat

Pasta
shells

DURUM WHEAT
Another large-grain wheat closely related to emmer is durum, or macaroni, wheat. It is grown widely today to provide the flour for pasta. It is not used for making bread because it has a low content of gluten - the substance that makes bread light and airy. Modern durum wheat has bigger grains as a result of intensive breeding.

Bread
wheat

Uncooked
whole-wheat
flour

BREAD WHEAT
Bread wheat is also a hybrid between emmer and wild goat grass and is the most widely grown modern wheat. Its large grains have a high gluten content which makes bread dough elastic and enables light, airy bread to be made.

White bread,
made from very
finely ground flour
that has been bleached

57

Potions and poisons

IN ANCIENT TIMES, plants were the main source of medicines. By trial and error, it was discovered that particular species could cure certain diseases. These plants were often grown in special gardens, and their details noted in plant reference books called herbals. Today many plants are still used in medicine. The chemicals they produce may be poisonous in large quantities, but small amounts can prove very useful in the treatment of some illnesses. The search for new medicines continues today, and every year pharmacologists examine thousands of plants from all over the world.

Aloe vera

Jojoba

MANDRAKE
The mandrake root, once used in medicines, sometimes looks almost human. It was usually pulled up by a dog, because, according to an old superstition, the root would shriek as it came out of the ground. Any human who heard the noise would die.

OUT OF THE EAST
In China, ginseng has been prized for about 5,000 years. The powdered root has a stimulant effect and can aid recovery from illness. Ginseng is grown commercially and is now sold all over the world.

Red ginseng root from Korea

Opium poppies growing in Turkey

Cosme preparati made fr aloe ve

COSMETIC EFFECT
Plants are often used in cosmetics for their pleasant smell or soothing oils. Two plants that are popular in today's cosmetics are jojoba and aloe vera. Both live in dry places and contain oils that help to keep skin soft.

THE OPIUM POP
For thousands of years opi poppies have been grown a source of drugs. Raw opi is the poppy's dried s It oozes out of the unri seed head after it h been scarred wit knife. Opium is us in the manufacture morphine, codei and heroin - dru which can be dead if misuse

Beans contain oil and poisonous ricin

Detail of a page from a 12th-century herbal

Agwensquidem decocosndos
Qudamucamellam eam uoc

Castor-oil plant

A DEADLY DOSE
The oil from the beans of the castor-oil plant has been used to purify the system since the days of the ancient Egyptians. The beans also contain rici one of the most potent poisons known. Ricin is s powerful that, if eaten, just one bean is enough kill an adult.

Leaves of the dumb cane

THE DUMB CANE
The name of this plant comes from its poisonous sap. If the sap is swallowed, it makes the mouth swell so much that talking becomes difficult.

DRINK OR DRUG?
The mescal cactus *Lophophora williamsii* contains a substance called mescaline which causes hallucinations and is used in the religious rituals of certain Mexican Indian tribes. The Mexican drink mescal is not derived from the mescal cactus *Lophophora*, but from another Mexican plant, *Agave tequilana*.

Mescal cactus

The drink mescal is made from the plant *Agave tequilana*

DEADLY BERRIES
The drug atropine, which is used in eye surgery and to treat stomach complaints, is derived from a very poisonous plant called belladonna, or deadly nightshade.

FROM COCA TO COCAINE
Many centuries ago, South American Indians discovered that chewing the leaves of the coca plant dulled pain and prevented tiredness. Coca leaves contain the drug cocaine. Although a valuable anaesthetic, cocaine can be dangerously addictive.

Coca leaves for sale

ca leaves

Foxglove

This group in India at the end of the 19th century are relaxing with a gin and tonic

Belladonna, or deadly nightshade

LP FOR E HEART
e leaves of the xglove contain gitalis, a sub- nce used to treat art conditions. In ge doses, it oduces palpitations d dizziness, but in aller doses, it helps e heart to beat more wly and strongly.

A CURE FOR MALARIA
Quinine, which is used in the treatment of malaria, is obtained from the bark of South American cinchona trees. Quinine is also used as a bitter flavor in tonic water, a drink which is commonly mixed with gin.

Cinchona leaves

The plant collectors

A 19th-century plant collector with his collection case, or vasculum

MANY OF THE PLANTS that have become common in gardens all over the world are, in fact, very far from home. Most fuchsias, for example, come originally from South America, wisteria from China and Japan, many azaleas from the Himalayas, and tulips from western and central Asia. These are just some of the thousands of plants that have been carried across the world by plant collectors. Plant collecting had its heyday in the 19th and early 20th centuries, as intrepid botanists traveled farther and farther afield in search of unknown plants. Some plant collectors experienced great hardships on their voyages to distant places - being shot at, caught in earthquakes, and attacked by wild animals. But despite all such adversities, the lure of making new discoveries spurred them on to explore some of the world's most remote and dangerous places.

Scutellaria tournefortii is named after its discoverer, Joseph Pitton de Tournefort

ROYAL MISSION
Joseph Pitton de Tournefort (1656-1708) was a botanist who was sent to the eastern Mediterranean by the French king Louis XIV. He returned with the specimens and seeds of over a thousand plants, many of which became garden favorites.

A 19th-century vasculum containing *Sarcococca hookerana*, a species of sweet box, one of many plants named by the Hookers

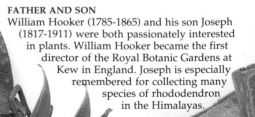

GOING EAST
The photograph above shows botanists on a plant-collecting expedition to China in the 1920s. This region of the world has been of great interest to botanists for many years, and expeditions made there today still discover new plant species. The photograph on the right shows a botanist on a modern plant-collecting expedition.

FATHER AND SON
William Hooker (1785-1865) and his son Joseph (1817-1911) were both passionately interested in plants. William Hooker became the first director of the Royal Botanic Gardens at Kew in England. Joseph is especially remembered for collecting many species of rhododendron in the Himalayas.

Leaves of
sycamore

Tradescant
father
and son

GOING WEST
John Tradescant and his son, also named John,
were English plantsmen. Tradescant the elder
collected in Russia, and Tradescant the younger
collected in America. The younger Tradescant
imported trees into Europe. These included the
tulip tree and the sycamore.

FIT FOR ROYALTY
Plant collecting is an ancient pursuit. This
Egyptian mural shows the earliest recorded
expedition, which took place in 1495 B.C.
Collectors brought back frankincense trees for
Queen Hatshepsut from the Horn of Africa.

Tradescantia - a
border plant named
after John Tradescant
the elder

…utifully preserved
…anical reference books

THE EMPRESS COLLECTOR
Empress Josephine, the wife of
Napoleon, created a unique garden at
her house at Malmaison with roses
brought from all around the world. At
the time France was at war with
Britain, but ships carrying the imperial
roses were allowed safe passage.

Looking at plants

PLANT COLLECTIONS are of two kinds – living plants and preserved specimens. The preserved specimens are mostly pressed and are kept in a herbarium where they can be examined by botanists. Collections of living plants are equally important and sometimes insure that rare plant species do not die out. Making your own collection of flowers and pressing them is a good way to learn about plants. However, you should not pick flowers that are growing wild in the countryside, as this prevents them from producing seeds. Some wildflower species are very rare and are protected by law; check with local authorities to find out what they are. If you want to try to grow your own plants, you can collect small amounts of seed or you can buy wildflower seed produced by plants that have been raised in nurseries. Growing your own plants gives you a chance to study them without harming plants in the wild.

Herbarium specimen sheet

Preserving bottle

Box containing dried specimen

HERB. HORT. REG. B

la echinacea
Forest, Lincs

Plant press

47819
HERB. HORT. BOT. REG. KEW.

Dendrobium (lindleyi) aggregatum Rol

Thailand   Menzies & July 89

BOTANIST'S COLLECTING EQUIPMENT
Specimens being collected for a herbarium are pressed and then mounted on a herbarium sheet with a label saying where and when they were found. The herbarium sheet can then be consulted by botanists wishing to study the plants in detail.

Pruning shears

Trowel

Sketchbook

Magnifying glass

LEARNING MORE ABOUT PLANTS
One of the best ways of finding out more about wildflowers is to draw or photograph them. If you draw them, you will notice many details about their structure, which will help you to identify the plant family. A magnifying glass can be useful for examining leaves and petals more closely. Collecting seeds and growing plants from them requires patience and care. Stored seeds should always be kept dry. Many seeds will germinate better if they are left in a refrigerator for a few weeks before planting. This cold period simulates the low winter temperatures they may experience in the wild. Large seeds, like those from sweet peas, germinate more quickly if they are first scratched, or "scarified," with sandpaper.

Scissors

Camera

Envelopes for collecting seed

PRESERVING SPECIMENS
Plants can be pressed with a simple screw press. The specimens are laid between two sheets of absorbent paper, which should be replaced with dry sheets every day or so. It can take a few weeks for specimens to dry out.

Top for plant press

Plant press

Screws for tightening plant press

Did you know?

AMANING FACTS

Bristlecone
pine tree

The oldest individual living plant is thought to be the bristlecone pine (*Pinus aristata*). One such plant has been dated at 4,900 years old, although a huge huon pine (*Dacrydium franklinii*) recently found in Tasmania may be older.

The orchid family has more species than any other flowering plant, with 25,000–30,000 species recognized, mostly in tropical regions. Orchids are found in every continent except for Antarctica and inhabit just about every type of environment except for extreme deserts and salt water.

Arctic lupine

The oldest seed known to botany comes from the North American Arctic lupine plant and is thought to be about 10,000 years old. The tendency of lupine seeds to be naturally preserved by the cold gave scientists the idea to place seeds in cold storage as stock for the future.

The fynbos, or evergreen bushland, of the Cape region in South Africa, contains one of the world's densest concentrations of plants within a small area. The east and north coasts around Cape Town are home to an amazing range of aloes, proteas, and ericas. There are an estimated 6,500 plant species in this tiny region—almost as many as on the entire continent of Europe.

Sphagnum moss, which is found in bogs and contributes to the formation of peat, can soak up more than 25 times its own dry weight in moisture.

Much less is known about small plants than large ones. Scientists estimate that they have identified 85–90 percent of flowering plants but only about 5 percent of the world's microscopic organisms.

The largest fruit is the pumpkin, which can weigh up to 1,130 lb (513 kg). Its close rival is the squash, which has been known to grow to 893 lb (405 kg).

The main ingredient in chocolate is the bean of the cacao tree, which grows in the rain forests of South America.

Proteas

Fossils of the still-existing ginkgo tree (*Ginkgo biloba*) date back some 160 million years. It first appeared at the time of the dinosaurs, during the Jurassic period. Today, extract from the bark and root of the tree is considered to have medicinal benefits for humans. The seed kernel of the tree is a delicacy in China.

The raffia palm (*Raffia ruffia*) has the largest leaves of any plant, measuring up to more than 66 ft (20 m) in length.

The banyan tree (*Ficus benghalensis*) has aerial roots that grow down from the tree's branches and eventually form new trunks. In this way, the banyan grows both upward and downward.

Japan values the chrysanthemum flower highly. The country has dedicated a whole day (September 9) to the flower, and the *feng shui* tradition teaches that the chrysanthemum brings laughter and happiness to a home.

Tulips were originally native to Turkey, Iran, Syria, and parts of Asia before being brought to Europe by traveling merchants in the 16th century. The Dutch were the first European nation to cultivate tulips, doing so in 1593. By 1633, the Dutch upper classes were so gripped by "tulip mania" that individual bulbs were changing hands for huge sums of money.

The farthest known distance traveled by a drift seed is that of a plant called Mary's bean (*Merremia discoidesperma*), which traveled 15,000 miles (24,150 km) from the Marshall Islands to the coast of Norway.

Orchid

QUESTIONS AND ANSWERS

The color of the cherry is key to its survival

Q Why are the fruits of the cherry plant red?

A The fruits of the cherry plant are bright red in color to attract birds to eat the fruit as food. The cherries contain seeds that have a hard protective covering to ensure that when they are eaten by birds, the seeds will pass through the digestive system of the creatures unharmed. In this way, the seeds are safely spread, and the plant ensures its own survival. Plants pollinated by insects are rarely red because insects, with the exception of butterflies, cannot see red.

Q Which plant is considered to be the most bizarre of all?

A *Welwitschia mirabilis*, from the Namibian desert, is one of the strangest plants in the world. Known to live for up to 2,000 years, it has a stumpy stem and just two straplike leaves, which grow nonstop throughout its life. As the plant ages, its leaves become twisted and gnarled and can eventually be many yards long. The leaves are tough and woody—an adaptation that helps protect them from being eaten or drying out. *Welwitschia* survives in a region where there is little rain but where fog rolls in from the sea. The plant's leaves gather moisture from the fog, helping it survive. *Welwitschia* does not grow flowers but produces seeds in cones.

Q What is the richest plant region of the world?

A South America holds an estimated 90,000 species. Brazil leads the world as the country with the greatest known number of plant species, at 56,000, followed by Colombia, with 35,000. Mexico, Venezuela, Ecuador, Bolivia, and Peru are not far behind. The proliferation of plant species in this part of the world is thought to be due to the moist habitat associated with its tropical rain forests, as well as the relatively recent arrival of humans.

Q Why do some tree leaves change color in the fall?

A As the days become colder and shorter, chlorophyll, the green pigment in the leaves, breaks down and flows back into the tree. Meanwhile, waste products, such as tannins, pass out into the leaves. This chemical change produces browns and reds in the colors of the leaves as they die. Trees that lose their leaves are deciduous.

Record Breakers

Smallest plant
• The world's smallest flowering plant is duckweed, (*Wolffia angusta*). A tablespoon can hold more than 100,000 plants, and each measures only 0.031 in (0.8 mm) long and 0.016 in (0.4 mm) wide.

Largest seed
• The largest seed produced by any plant is that of the coco-de-mer (*Lodoicea maldivica*) from the Seychelles. This palm, also known as the double coconut tree, produces seeds that weigh up to 50 lb (23 kg) and take up to 10 years to grow into a tree.

Tallest tree
• The Mendocino coast redwood (*Sequoia sempervirens*), found in California, is the tallest tree in the world. The maximum height it has reached is 367.5 ft (112.01 m).

Duckweed

Weltwitschia mirabilis

Plant classification

THE PLANT KINGDOM is divided into different groups and contains about 400,000 separate species that we know about. The majority of plant organisms belong to the flowering plant family called angiosperms. The groups shown here cover all of the main plant classifications.

Ginkgo

Liverwort

Most liverworts have leaves but they can also be flat and leafless

GINKGO
The ginkgo, or maidenhair, tree is native to China. It is related to conifers but it has many unusual features, which is why it is classified in a group of its own. Unlike most conifers, ginkgos are deciduous, and they have fan-shaped leaves.

MOSSES AND LIVERWORTS
Mosses and liverworts belong to a group called the bryophytes, which number 14,000 species. These small plants usually grow in shaded, damp places. They first appeared around 425 million years ago and contributed to the formation of coal and peat.

FLOWERING PLANTS

Flowering plants, or angiosperms, constitute about 300,000 species, the vast majority of plants. A flower is a specialized part of the plant and develops into a fruit, which contains one or more seeds housed in ovaries. These seeds must be pollinated and dispersed to ensure the continuation of each species. There are two types of flowering plants: monocots and dicots.

Wheat

Rose

Monocots have a single cotyledon, or seedleaf. Their adult leaves are often long and narrow, with parallel veins. Monocots include cereals, such as wheat; some vegetables, such as leeks; some fruits, such as pineapples; and also orchids and lilies. They number about 55,000 species.

Dicots are plants whose seeds have two cotyledons, or seedleaves. Their adult leaves usually have a network of veins around a central midrib. Dicots total at least 250,000 species, and they include most shrubs and all the world's broadleaved trees.

Dicot plants often have woody stems.

Pineapple

Leek

Cabbage

Cactus

CLUBMOSSES

Clubmoss

Clubmosses, or lycopodophytes, existed as far back as 430 million years ago. Today's clubmosses are small, with overlapping leaves and creeping stems, but some prehistoric clubmosses grew into giant trees. Clubmosses reproduce by growing spores.

~~FE~~RNS

~~Al~~so known as pteridophytes, ferns include around 12,000 species and ~~l~~ive in damp environments, such as forests. Fern leaves are called fronds ~~an~~d carry spores on the underside. These spores produce tiny plants ~~tha~~t reproduce in turn, giving rise to the next generation of adult ferns.

~~C~~ONIFERS

~~Thi~~s group of about 550 species ~~is~~ mostly comprised of large ~~ev~~ergreen trees. Conifers can ~~ph~~otosynthesize even in winter ~~an~~d are often characterized by ~~ne~~edle-shaped leaves. This ~~gro~~up includes pines, firs, ~~sp~~ruces, cedars, cypresses, ~~an~~d yews.

Pine

CYCADS

Cycads, which are gymnosperms, grow in the tropics. Although similar in appearance, they are not related to palms. Abundant in the Jurassic period, there are now just 100 species left. Their attractive leaves make them popular garden plants.

Cycad

HORSETAILS

These ancient plants are called sphenophytes. Around 300 million years ago they reached heights of 49 ft (15 m). Today there are only about 35 species left. This family is closely related to the fern group.

Vast horsetail forests once grew on Earth.

Horsetail

Cones are produced during the summer months.

Weltwitschia mirabilis, also known as the tumboa

GNETOPHYTES

Cone-bearing desert plants, or gnetophytes, resemble flowering plants in many ways and were once thought to be a missing link between conifers and angiosperms. There are about 70 species in existence today.

Find out more

I<small>F YOU WOULD LIKE TO</small> find out more about plants, you won't have to search far. Indeed, you only have to look around you. Go exploring in your own garden or start a window box. Armed with a plant identification handbook, take a walk in your local park or nature preserve, where you will find plenty of specimens to admire and study. For more exotic species and a wealth of information, visit a botanical garden. To check out ancient plant fossils, take a trip to a natural history museum. Flower markets can also be an interesting and colorful experience.

If an area of land is privately owned, always seek permission from the owner before exploring.

BOTANICAL GARDENS
A botanical garden is dedicated to plants from around the world. Rare and exotic species are cultivated, often in specially controlled environments such as greenhouses. Desert plants, for example, must be kept in hot, dry climate for survival.

GO WILD
To see plants in a completely natural setting, just head for your local nature preserve (bring an adult with you). Spring is a good time to observe budding flowers and new shoots. Few sights compare to the vivid beauty of a meadow in midsummer bloom with wildflowers.

Wildflowers should not be picked, as this would disturb the natural environment

This garden pansy will lose some of its color as it dries.

When the flower is dry, write the plant name and date picked on the sheet of paper.

COLLECTING DRIED FLOWERS
Pick a flower in full bloom. Detach the flower head and leaves and place them flat on a sheet of blotting paper. Fold and enclose the sheet between the pages of a heavy book and allow to dry for a few weeks.

Places to Visit

MISSOURI BOTANICAL GARDEN, ST. LOUIS, MISSOURI
Features a variety of themed gardens, including the largest Japanese garden in North America, plus the Climatron, the world's first geodesic dome greenhouse.

NEW ORLEANS BOTANICAL GARDEN, NEW ORLEANS, LOUISIANA
An Art Deco botanical garden focusing on the plants of the Gulf South.

DESERT BOTANICAL GARDEN, PHOENIX, ARIZONA
Plants of the desert are the centerpiece here. Visit Plants and People of the Sonoran Trail, where visitors can twist agave fibers into twine, and four other trails.

NEW YORK BOTANICAL GARDEN, BRONX, NEW YORK
Features a Victorian-era greenhouse, the Enid A. Haupt Conservatory, and a children's garden.

WOODLAND WALKS
There are many official nature walks that choose specific routes best suited to the time of year. The organized walk below follows a path that takes ramblers through the first colorful crop of springtime bluebells.

ORNAMENTAL BUNCHES
A bouquet of flowers doesn't have to fade away. Its beauty can be preserved by taking it out of water and keeping it in a safe place until each stem has dried. Tie with a ribbon and place in a vase or on the wall.

This bunch of flowers was purchased at a flower market.

IN YOUR OWN BACK YARD
If you have a yard, this is the best place to find out more about plants. Using a notebook, you can log the growth and development of various species through the seasons. You can also grow your own plants.

ROOM WITH A VIEW
If you don't have access to a yard, window boxes make very rewarding miniature gardens. Flowers and herbs can be grown in any container and placed on a window ledge. Another way to grow plants outside is to cut an opening in a large bag of compost and use it as a soil bed.

Sunflower seeds should ideally be planted in May.

USEFUL WEB SITES

- All about gardening for kids, with great links:
  www.kidsgardening.com
- What can you do to help trees in the city? Visit this site for ideas:
  www.treesaremyfriends.org
- Funky gardening tips for beginners:
  www.yougrowgirl.com
- Missouri Botanical Gardens online:
  mbgnet.mobot.org
- Science projects and fun facts about botany:
  www.nbii.gov/disciplines/botany/science.html

Glossary

ACHENE A dry, one-seeded fruit. Plants in the buttercup family all have achenes.

ALGA A simple nonflowering plant that usually lives in water. Algae include seaweeds and many microscopic species.

ANGIOSPERM A flowering plant. Unlike gymnosperms, angiosperms grow their seeds inside a protective case called an ovary, which develops to form a fruit.

ANNUAL A plant that completes its life cycle within the growing season of one year

ANTHER The tip of a flower's stamen containing pollen

AXIL The angle between the upper part of a stem and a leaf or branch. Buds develop in the axil.

AXIS The main stem or root in a plant

BIENNIAL A plant that has two growing seasons. The seed is sown in the first year and flowers and fruits in its second year. The plant then dies.

BOTANY The scientific study of plants

BRACT A small leaflike flap that grows just beneath a flower

BUD The first visible sign of a new limb of a plant, or the protective case that encloses a flower that is still growing inside

BULB An underground stem that stores food inside layers of fleshy scales. Plants use bulbs to survive drought or cold.

Stem and leaves sprouting from bulb

BULBIL A small bud that grows into an independent plant

BURR The prickly seedcase of some plants

CALYX The ring of sepals that protects a flower bud. The calyx often falls off when the flower blooms.

CARPEL The female organ of a flower, consisting of the stigma, the style, and the ovary

Daffodil bulbs

Green alga, or seaweed

CELL The smallest possible unit of living matter, visible only under a microscope and consisting of a nucleus surrounded by cytoplasm and bound by a cell wall

CHLOROPHYLL The green pigment present in all plants and algae and involved in the process of photosynthesis

CHLOROPLAST A microscopic green structure, containing chlorophyll, that captures energy from sunlight inside plant cells

CLIMBER A plant that grows upward and outward, attaching itself to structures such as walls and fences

COROLLA The ring of petals in a flower

COTYLEDON A specialized leaf that is prepacked inside a seed. Cotyledons often look quite different from ordinary leaves.

DECIDUOUS A plant that loses its leaves seasonally

DICOT A plant whose seeds have two cotyledons. A dicot's leaves are often broad and have veins arranged in a network.

EMBRYO A young plant in its earliest stages of development

ENDOSPERM A supply of food that is stored inside a seed. The endosperm fuels the seedling's early growth.

EVERGREEN A plant that keeps its leaves year round, such as pines and firs

FILAMENT The stalk of a stamen, which supports the anther

FLORET A small flower that forms part of a composite flower, or flowerhead

GERMINATION When a seed begins to sprout and grow

GYMNOSPERM A plant whose seeds do not develop inside an ovary. Most gymnosperms are coniferous trees.

HARDY A plant that can withstand extremes of temperature, such as cold and frost

MONOCOT One of the two divisions of angiosperms. Monocots, or monocotyledons, are plants whose leaves have parallel veins. The other division of angiosperms is dicots.

MULTICELLULAR Comprised of more than one cell

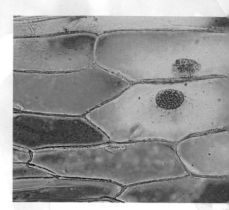

A microscopic view of typical plant cells

NECTAR Naturally occurring sweet liquid found in the glands of many flowers

OVARY A female reproductive organ, which encloses fertilized seeds

OVULE A collection of female cells that form a seed after they have been fertilized by pollen

PAPPUS A ring or parachute of very fine hair that grows above a seed and helps it to be dispersed by the wind

PARACHUTE Any structure that aids the spread of seeds by the wind, such as a pappus

PARASITE An organism that lives in or on another organism, or host, from which it takes food and energy without giving anything back in return

PERENNIAL A plant that lasts or flowers for more than two years

PERIANTH The part of a flower made up of the calyx and the corolla together

PETAL A leafy flap in a flower, often brightly colored to attract animal pollinators

The strawberry plant is a dicot.

PHLOEM A system of cells that carries nutrients throughout a plant

PIGMENT A colored chemical used by plants to collect light. One pigment, chlorophyll, makes plants look green.

PLANTLET A young plant, sometimes attached to its parent

PHOTOSYNTHESIS The process by which plants generate their own food, occurring when a green pigment called chlorophyll reacts with sunlight, carbon dioxide, and water to make carbohydrates, water, and oxygen

PLUMULE The embryo shoot in a seed

POLLEN Microscopic grains containing male sex cells. Pollen is produced by the anthers of flowers.

POLLINATION The process by which pollen is carried from one flower to another. The male pollen fertilizes the female ovule and creates a seed. Insects and animals often carry pollen between flowering plants, or it can be blown by the wind.

RECEPTACLE The part of a plant that contains the flower, or, in flowerless plants, the reproductive organs or spores

RHIZOME A creeping underground stem. Rhizomes often sprout leaves as they push their way through the ground.

ROOT The part of a plant that anchors it to a solid surface, such as soil, and absorbs water and nutrients

RUNNER A stem that produces new plants by growing across the ground and sprouting roots

The bamboo plant is a monocot.

Poppy seeds carried on the wind

SEED A tough structure used by plants to reproduce. A seed contains a young plant, or embryo, together with all the food reserves it needs to start life on its own.

SEPAL A leafy flap that protects a flower while it is still a bud. Sepals often fall off when the flower opens.

SHOOT The parts of a plant above ground, including its stems, leaves, and flowers

SPADIX A fleshy spike of flowers

SPATHE A leaflike hood that partly encloses a flowerhead

SPECIES A group of plants or other living things that look similar and that normally breed together in the wild

SPORE A single-celled reproductive unit of some organisms

SPUR A flowering or fruit-bearing branch that shoots out from an existing plant

STAMEN The pollen-producing part of a flower, consisting of a filament and an anther

STARCH The main food type stored in a plant. Chemically known as a carbohydrate, this food contains vital energy reserves.

STEM The part of a plant that carries the leaves. Also known as a stalk, the stem transports water and food from the roots to the rest of the plant.

STOMA An opening through which gases enter and leave the green part of a plant

TENDRIL A threadlike part of a plant that grows outward and wraps around nearby objects, helping the plant stay upright

TAPROOT A main root growing down

TEPAL A flap around a flower that works like a combination of a sepal and a petal

TENDER A plant that is sensitive to the cold

TESTA A hard shell of coating around a seed

TRANSPIRATION The movement of water through a plant. Water is taken up by the roots, and evaporates through pores in the leaves.

A variegated ivy leaf

TUBER A swelling or lump that forms in a root or stem and usually contains valuable food reserves for the rest of the plant. A potato is a tuber.

UMBEL An umbrella-shaped flowerhead

WHORL A collection of leaves, sepals, or petals growing in a circle around a plant stem

VARIEGATION Streaky or mottled, with contrasting colors. In plants, variegated leaves are caused by differences in the pigments across the leaf.

VEGETATION The plants found in a particular habitat or environment

XYLEM A system of cells that carries water through a plant. In shrubs and trees, toughened xylem cells form wood.

ZYGOTE A fertilized egg

Index

Acknowledgments

The publisher would like to thank:
Brinsley Burbidge, Valerie Whalley, John Lonsdale, Milan Swaderlig, Andrew McRobb, Marilyn Ward, and Pat Griggs of the Royal Botanic Gardens, Kew, England. Arthur Chater at the Natural History Museum.
David Burnie for consultancy.
Dave King for special photography on pages 8–9.
Fred Ford and Mike Pilley at Radius for artwork.

Picture credits
t=top, b=bottom, m=middle, l=left, r=right
A-Z Botanical: 55m
Heather Angel/Biofotos: 43tm; 49ml
V. Angel/Daily Telegraph Colour Library: 39bm
Australian High Commission: 24tr; 57tr
A.N.T./NHPA: 25mr
J. and M. Bain/NHPA: 11bl
G.I. Bernard/Oxford Scientific Films: 7tl; 46br
G.I. Bernard/NHPA: 15tr; 18mr; 36m; 40mr
Deni Bown/Oxford Scientific Films: 64bc
Bridgeman Art Library: 55mb; 58br
Brinsley Burbidge/Royal Botanic Gardens, Kew: 50bm; 58m
M.Z. Capell/ZEFA: 10tr
James H. Carmichael/NHPA: 53br
Gene Cox/Science Photo Library: 7m
Stephen Dalton/NHPA: 19tr; 22ml; 30tl; 36tr; 40ml
P. Dayanandan/Science Photo Library: 9tl
Jack Dermid/Oxford Scientific Films: 32br
Dr. Dransfield/Royal Botanic Gardens, Kew 45
Mary Evans Picture Library: 44 tl; 46bl; 48ml; 56tl, tr; 60tr; 61br; 62tm
Patrick Fagot/NHPA: 71bl
Robert Francis/South American Pictures: 54tl
Linda Gamlin: 27mr; 29bm
Brian Hawkes/NHPA: 23tl
Hulton Picture Library: 42tl
E.A. Janes/NHPA: 28bl; 68br
Peter Lillie/Oxford Scientific Films: 65b; 67b
Patrick Lynch/Science Photo Library: 6tm; 8br
Mansell Collection: 8bl; 59bm
Marion Morrison/South American Pictures: 59m
Peter Newark's Western Americana: 52br
Oxford Scientific Films: 66tl
Brian M. Rogers/Biofotos: 46bm
Royal Botanic Gardens, Kew: 16tl; 43tl; 60m; 61m
John Shaw/NHPA: 9tr; 64tl, br
Survival Anglia: 7tl
Silvestris Fotoservice/FLPA: 65tl
John Walsh/Science Photo Library: 15tl
M.I. Walker/NHPA: 70tr
J. Watkins/Frank Lane Picture Agency: 50bl
Alan Williams: 68tr
Rogers Wilmshurst/Frank Lane: 26tr
David Woodfall/NHPA: 68c
Steven Wooster: 69tr
Jacket images: Front: Bill Ross/Corbis, b; Peter Lillie/OSF, tl; Mary Evans Picture Library, tcr.
Illustrations by: Sandra Pond and Will Giles: 12–13, 17, 38
Picture research by: Angela Jones and Lorna Ainger